READ WELL
Plus

Judy Moody Saves the World!

Teacher's Guide

Unit 24

Review

Note: See New and Important Objectives on page 2 for a complete list of skills taught and reviewed.

Critical Foundations in Primary Reading

Marilyn Sprick, Ann Watanabe, Karen Akiyama-Paik, and Shelley V. Jones

Sopris West®
EDUCATIONAL SERVICES

A Cambium Learning® Company

BOSTON, MA · LONGMONT, CO

ISBN 13-digit: 978-1-60218-547-0
ISBN 10-digit: 1-60218-547-6

6   7   8   9   RRDHRBVA   14   13   12   11   10

167071/1-10

Table of Contents
Unit 24
Judy Moody Saves the World!

How to Teach the Lessons

End of the Unit

Letter Sounds and Combinations

Cumulative Review of *Read Well 1* Sounds and Combinations (Ss, Ee, ee, Mm, Aa, Dd, th, Nn, Tt, Ww, Ii, Th, Hh, Cc, Rr, ea, sh, Sh, Kk, -ck, oo, ar, wh, Wh, ĕ, -y as in fly, Ll, Oo, Bb, all, Gg, Ff, Uu, er, oo as in book, Yy, a schwa, Pp, ay, Vv, Qq, Jj, Xx, or, Zz, a_e, -y as in baby, i_e, ou, ow as in cow, ch, Ch, ai, igh, o_e, ir) and:

Unit 2	Unit 3		Unit 5	Unit 6
aw /aw/ **Paw** Voiced	**ew** /ōō/ **Crew** Voiced	**ue** /ōō/ **Blue** Voiced	**ow** /ōōō/ **Snow** Voiced (Long)	**ge** /j/ **Page** Voiced

(Unit 3 continued) **u_e** /ōō/ **Flute** Bossy E Voiced

Unit 6	Unit 7		Unit 8		Unit 10
-dge /j/ **Badge** Voiced	**ci** /sss/ **Circle** Unvoiced	**ce** /sss/ **Center** Unvoiced	**kn** /nnn/ **Knee** Voiced	**ph** /fff/ **Phone** Unvoiced	**oa** /ōōō/ **Boat** Voiced (Long)

Unit 11		Unit 12		Unit 13
oi /oi/ **Point** Voiced	**ea** /ĕĕĕ/ **Bread** Voiced (Short)	**gi** /j/ **Giraffe** Voiced	**au** /au/ **Astronaut** Voiced	**oy** /oy/ **Boy** Voiced

Affixes (including morphographs—affixes taught with meaning) and Open Syllables

Cumulative Review of *Read Well 1* Affixes (-ed, -en, -es, -ing, -ly, -s, -y, -tion) and:

Unit 2	Unit 3		Unit 5	Unit 6
re- **Means again** as in reread	**un-** **Means not** as in unhappy	**ex-** as in excited	**o** Open syllable /ō/ as in open and moment	**-ful** **Means full of** as in colorful

(Unit 6) **bi-** **Means two** as in bicycle

Unit 7	Unit 8	Unit 11	Unit 12	Unit 13	
de- as in detective	**-able** as in comfortable	**i** Open syllable /ī/ as in silence and pilot	**be-** as in before	**-ous** as in enormous	**dis-** as in discover

Unit 14		Unit 15		Unit 16	
-al as in animal	**-ible** as in flexible	**-or** **Means one who** as in actor	**-ment** as in apartment	**-ic** as in scientific	**pre-** **Means before** as in preview

Unit 17		Unit 18		Unit 19	
-ity as in activity	**-sion** as in permission	**-ness** as in fairness	**-less** **Means without** as in helpless	**in-** as in insert	**im-** **Means not** as in impossible

Introduction
Judy Moody Saves the World!

Story Notes

Judy Moody Saves the World! Meet Judy Moody, a spunky third-grade heroine, and her little brother, Stink. As the story begins, Judy wants to win the Crazy Strips Band-Aid design contest so that cuts and scrapes everywhere will be covered with her winning design. But after her science class studies the rain forest and endangered species, Judy sets her sights higher and starts a crusade to save the world.

Recommended Read Alouds

The *Read Well 2* suggested Read Alouds enhance small group instruction—providing opportunities to further build background knowledge and vocabulary.

> **CAUTION**
> **(Reminder)**
> Do not read the Read Aloud recommendations during small group instruction. Reserve this time for students to read.

Stink: The Incredible Shrinking Kid by Megan McDonald

Fiction • Narrative

Judy's little brother tells his own story. Already the shortest kid in his second grade class, he seems to be shrinking, at least according to the morning measurements made by his bossy big sister. Stink tries everything to grow taller, from spiking his hair to eating vast quantities of peas.

Read Well Connections

As students read about Judy Moody, they'll enjoy hearing the perspective of her younger brother. Encourage students to compare the stories, noting differences between the main characters.

NOTE FROM THE AUTHORS

> **CONNECTIONS: SOCIAL STUDIES**
> This unit demonstrates how one person can make the world a better place to live. Students learn right along with Judy about rain forest destruction and endangered species. The book also contains tips for recycling and reusing materials.

New and Important Objectives
A Research-Based Reading Program

Phonics
Cumulative Letter Sounds and Combinations
Review • Ss, Ee, ee, Mm, Aa, Dd, th, Nn, Tt, Ww, Ii, Th, Hh, Cc, Rr, ea, sh, Sh, Kk, -ck, oo, ar, wh, Wh, ĕ, -y (as in fly), Ll, Oo, Bb, all, Gg, Ff, Uu, er, oo (as in book), Yy, a (schwa), Pp, ay, Vv, Qq, Jj, Xx, or, Zz, a_e, -y (as in baby), i_e, ou, ow (as in cow), ch, Ch, ai, igh, o_e, ir, aw, ew, ue, u_e, ow (as in snow), ge, -dge, ci, ce, kn, ph, oa, oi, ea (as in bread), gi, au, oy

Cumulative Affixes, Morphographs, and Open Syllables
Review • -ed, -en, -er, -es, -est, -ing, -ly, -s, -y, -tion, re-, un-, ex-, o (as in open), -ful, bi-, de-, -able, i (as in silence), be-, -ous, dis-, -al, -ible, -or, -ment, -ic, pre-, -ity, -sion, -ness, -less, in-, im-

☆ New Abbreviations
Ph.D, CEO

☆ New Contractions
c'mon, how's, it'll, we'd

☆ New Proper Nouns
◆ Adam, Beatles, Blackwell, Brad, Brazil, Bullwinkle, Chesapeake Bay, County Parks Department, Dickson, Frank Pearl, Frank's, Hailey, Heather ◆ Hershey's, Jessica Finch, Jessica's, John Lennon, Judy Moody, Judy's, Julia, Laura Ingalls Wilder ◆ Leo, Lucy, Luna Two, Margaret Mead, Mr. Todd's, Ms. Stickley, Paul McCartney, Picasso, Randi, Ranger Piner, Ranger Rick magazine, Scarlett O'Cherry, Screamin' Mimi's, Siberian, Sleeping Beauty ◆ Sloppy Joes, Smithsonian, Social Studies, Stephanie, Stink's, T.P. Club, Toady, Toady's, Virginia Dare School

☆ New Pattern Words
bare, baring, beaches, bloomp ◆ boom ◆ bum, chance ◆ chin, clomp, clomped ◆ cone ◆ core, cure, fame ◆ fink, fond, freak, freaks, fridge, grind, grinding, grouch, grouchier, grouchy, heal, healing ◆ jugs, lice, louse ◆ nail, peel, peeling, peels ◆ pill, pond ◆ purse, raid, raided, rung, scum, sheesh, shone, smoosh, smooshed, sow, spewed, spy, spying, squeak, squeaking, squint, sting, theme, wailed

Known Pattern Words With Affixes • beaches, blinked, blinking, caps, cards, cares, cents, chewing, clapping, costs, crabs, crushed, cutting, draws, dumped, flags, frames, glued, grabbing, grounds, halls, harmful, hater, hissed, holder, hooting, itchy, kicks, leaky, malls, masks, misses, moods, panted, pasting, pig's, pigs', piling, plopped, prouder, racing, raising, rejoin, replace, replacing, scraped, shacking, shining, snapping, sneaked, sneezing, socks, spices, squirmed, stealing, stepping, stinking, stomps, straws, tanks, throws ◆ toadly ◆ toadster, tricked, whooping, winked, winking

☆ New Compound and Hyphenated Words
award-winning, band-aids ◆ bathroom, bathtub, big-eared, brainstorm ◆ classmates, cupboard ◆ driveway, eggshells, flashlight ◆ French-fry, goldfish ◆ gumball ◆ high-fived, hillside, humankind, lawsuits, leaf-cutter, leapfrog, lipstick, litterbugs, lunchroom, mailbox, makeup, ninety-eight, old-fashioned, papier-mâché, pillbuggy, prize-winning ◆ redwoods, rollerblades ◆ runners-up ◆ seashell, self-portraits, sendoff, shoreline, smartypants, solar-powered ◆ spotlight ◆ stamp-collecting, stinkbug, swallowtail, third-graders, thirty-eight, tiptoed, toadkind ◆ toadnapping ◆ T-shirt ◆ twenty-eight, twenty-four, twenty-one, twenty-seven ◆ uproar, walkie-talkies ◆ weekend, workbooks

---

* **Known Pattern Words With Affixes, Known Tricky Words With Affixes,** and **Known Multisyllabic Words With Affixes** have base words students have previously read. The words are new in this unit because they have not been previously read with the affix.

☆ = New in this unit

◆ = Words that are not introduced in the exercises before they are read in the storybook

Phonics (continued)

★Other New Multisyllabic Words

absent, accept, acid ◆ acorn, adhesive, affects, agua ◆ alien, anaconda, ankles, appointment, aquarium, army, assembly, awareness, bandage ◆ batty, beady, belfry, belfries, bother, brownie, cafeteria ◆ carton ◆ cartons, cassowary, catalog, catalogs, certificate, certificates, complained, complaining, complicated, concerned, confess, confessed, cranky ◆ cricketty, crummy, cursive ◆ cutters ◆ dentist, deserving, dictionary, donated, elbow, elbows, emergency, envy, erase, eraser, erosion, extremely, fanatic, funeral, garbologist, gazillion, gazillions, global, gooey, gremlin, hanger, hangers ◆ icketty, igloo, isopod, isopods ◆ jacket, kiddo, kindergarten, kindling, lentil, lentils, licey, lima, littering, lollipop, lunatic, mascot, mention, multipurpose, mushy, operation, outrageous, ozone, participants, pastels ◆ perfume, plunger, pollution, popsicle, positive, principal, punishment ◆ quarter, reflex, reflexes, represent, rhino, rubbish, silence, sister's, sluggy, smiley, spacious, specimen, squishy, stubborn, thirsty, total, traitor, ucky, universe, wrapper

*Known Multisyllabic Words With Affixes •

adopted, adopts, announcement, announcements, bananas, beetle's, believing, bubbles, capitals, collecting, collection, contribution, decayed, depends, development, disagreement, disappearing, efforts, enclosed, entering, envelopes, extremely, featured, feeders, holders, jealousy, magazines, marker, pajamas, pencils, pencil's, presented, rescued, teachers', teenagers, tigers, vampires, winners

★New Tricky Words

annual, biannual, casual, chorus, chrysalis, crustacean, crustaceans, crystal, design, designs, double, gonna, monarch, pencilvania, presidential

*Known Tricky Words With Affixes •

appreciation, behalf, curtains, dying, honorable, recycled, straighter, tomorrow's

★New Creature Names

Cicindela dorsalis dorsalis, Cinderella beetle, Dismal Swamp shrew, dung beetle, elderberry longhorn beetle ◆ hard-headed hornbill, Hercules beetle, leatherback sea turtle, monkeyface mussels, nocturnal aye-ayes, northeast beach tiger beetle, orange-foot pimpleback pearlmussel shell, pimplebacks, puma, pumas, Shenandoah salamander, shiny pigtoe, shortnose sturgeon, ◆ tropical treehoppers, two-toed sloths, Virginia fringed mountain snail

---

Fluency

Accuracy, Expression, Phrasing, Rate

Vocabulary

New • annoy, appreciation, batty, budge, complicated, concerned, confess, contribution, endangered species, environment, global warming, good cause, heal, ignore, inspiration, mascot, mention, mood, moody, original, outrageous, ozone, reflex, ruin, settled, stubborn, theme, traitor, uproar

Review • algae, ancient, appreciate, approximately, brag, brilliant, composting, confused, conserve, control, creative, creature, curious, destroy, determined, dinosaur, discouraged, distressed, ecosystem, endangered, extinct, frustrated, habitat, honor, imaginative, impossible, jealous, oxygen, permission, planet, popular, pout, practical, pretend, protect, recycle, responsible, summoned, thrilled, trade, upset, waste

Reviewed in Context • approximately, absolutely, ancient, brag, brilliant, cause, commotion, community, composting, congratulate, conserve, control, creative, creature, decay, destroy, dinosaur, disappointed, ecosystem, endangered, energy, eternal, expect, extinct, fascinating, globe, habitat, honor, imagination, inventor, jealous, legend, natural, nature, opinion, owe, oxygen, pant, peer, perfect, permission, planet, practical, pretend, prey, protect, protected, prove, recycle, reuse, survive, temperature, trade, unless, upset

Idioms and Expressions

New • crack someone up, fall for, green with envy, on behalf of, stick your neck out

Review • get rid of, save the day

Comprehension

Unit Genres

　　Fiction • Imaginative

Comprehension Processes

　　Build Knowledge: Factual, Procedural, Conceptual

Day	1	2	3	4	5	6	7	8	9	10	11	12
Remember												
Defining												
Identifying (recalling)	S,C	S,C	S	S,C	S,C	S,C	S	S	S	S,C	S,C	S,C
Using												
Understand												
Defining (in your own words)	S	S	S,C	C		S		S	S,C			C
Describing	S	S					S			S		C
Explaining (rephrasing)	S	S	S	S	S,C	S,C	S	S	S,C	S	S,C	S
Illustrating	C	C	C		C	C	C	C	C	C	C	
Sequencing												
Summarizing		S,C	S	S	S	S	S	S,C	S,C	S,C	S	S
Using	S	S	S,C	S,C	C	S,C	C	S	S,C	S,C	S,C	S,C
Visualizing												
Apply												
Demonstrating				S								
Explaining (unstated)	S,C		S	S	S	S	C	S	S	S	S	C
Illustrating			C	C	C	C	C	C	C	C	C	
Inferring	S	S	S	S,C	S	S	S,C	S,C	S	S,C	S	C
Making Connections (relating)		S		S	S			S	S		S	
Predicting	S	S		S	S	S		S	S	S		
Using	S	S	S	S	S	S	S,C	S	S,C	S	S	
Analyze												
Classifying					S		S					
Comparing/Contrasting												
Distinguishing Cause/Effect	C										C	
Drawing Conclusions	S		S		S	S	S	S	S	S		S
Inferring			S									
Evaluate												
Making Judgments		S	S				S		S			
Responding (personal)	C	C	C	S		S,C		C	C	C	S,C	
Create												
Generating Ideas	S,C	S,C	C	C		C	S,C	S,C	C	S,C	C	C

E = Exercise, S = Storybook, C = Comprehension & Skill

Comprehension (continued)

Skills and Strategies

Day	1	2	3	4	5	6	7	8	9	10	11	12
Priming Background Knowledge											S	
Setting a Purpose for Reading	S	S	S	S		S	S	S	S		S	
Answering Questions	S	S	S	S	S	S	S	S	S	S	S,C	
Asking Questions				C			C					C
Visualizing												
Comprehension Monitoring/Fix Ups												
Does it Make Sense?	C	C		C	C	C	C			C	C	
Looking Back												
Restating												
Summarizing												
Main Idea										C	S	
Retelling												
Supporting Details										C		S
Understanding Text Structure												
Title, Author, Illustrator	S	S	S	S	S	S	S	S	S	S	S	
Fact or Fiction												
Genre (Classifying)												
Narrative												
Setting												C
Main Character/Traits (Characterization)	C	S	S					C				
Goal	S	S	S									C
Problem/Solution		S	S	S		S			S			
Action/Events/Sequence				C						C	S,C	C
Outcome/Conclusion												
Lesson/Author's Message												
Expository												
Subject/Topic												
Heading												
Supporting Details (Facts/Information)			S	S	C	S			S	C		S
Main Idea										C	S	
Using Graphic Organizers												
Chart												
Diagram (labeling)												
Hierarchy (topic/detail)										C		
K-W-L												
Map (locating, labeling)												
Matrix (compare/contrast)												C
Sequence (linear, cycle, cause and effect)	C			C	C		C		C		C	
Story Map												
Web												

E = Exercise, S = Storybook, C = Comprehension & Skill

Comprehension (continued)

Study Skills

Day	1	2	3	4	5	6	7	8	9	10	11	12
Alphabetical Order												
Following Directions	C											
Locating Information		S,C		S						S	C	
Note Taking			S									
Previewing												
Reviewing		S	S	S	S	S	S	S	S	S	S	
Test Taking					C	C						C
Using Glossary												
Using Table of Contents	S	S										
Viewing	S			S	S	S	S	S	S	S	S	
Verifying												

Writing in Response to Reading

Day	1	2	3	4	5	6	7	8	9	10	11	12
Sentence Completion	C	C	C	C		C	C	C	C	C	C	
Making Lists		C	C	C	C		C					
Sentence Writing			C	C	C	C	C	C	C	C	C	C
Story Retell/Summary												
Fact Summary										C		
Paragraph Writing								C		C		C
Report Writing												
Open-Ended Response												
Creative Writing	C	C	C	C	C	C	C	C	C	C	C	

Writing Traits

(Addressed within the context of Writing in Response to Reading)

Day	1	2	3	4	5	6	7	8	9	10	11	12
Ideas and Content												
Elaborating/Generating	C	C	C	C		C	C	C	C	C	C	
Organization												
Introduction												
Topic Sentence										C		
Supporting Details										C		
Sequencing												
Word Choice												
Sophisticated Words (Tier 2 and 3)	C	C	C	C		C	C	C	C	C	C	
Conventions												
Capital	C	C	C	C	C	C	C	C	C	C	C	C
Ending Punctuation	C	C	C	C	C	C	C	C	C	C	C	C
Other (commas, quotation marks)												
Presentation												
Handwriting	C	C	C	C	C	C	C	C	C	C	C	C
Neatness	C	C	C	C	C	C	C	C	C	C	C	C

E = Exercise, S = Storybook, C = Comprehension & Skill

Daily Lesson Planning

LESSON PLAN FORMAT

Teacher-Directed 45 Minutes		Independent Teacher-Directed, as needed
Lesson Part 1 (Phonological Awareness, Phonics, Fluency, Comprehension) 15–20 Minutes	**Lesson Part 2** (Vocabulary, Fluency, Comprehension) 20–25 Minutes	**Lesson Part 3** (Vocabulary, Fluency, Comprehension) 15–20 Minutes
• Exercises	• Unit and/or Story Opener • Vocabulary • Interactive Story Reading • Short Passage Practice Timed Readings	• Story Reading With Partner or Whisper Reading • Comprehension and Skill Activities

HOMEWORK

Read Well Homework (blackline masters of new *Read Well 2* passages) provides an opportunity for children to celebrate accomplishments with parents. Homework should be sent home on routine days.

ORAL READING FLUENCY ASSESSMENT

Upon completion of this unit, assess each student and proceed to Unit 25, as appropriate.

WRITTEN ASSESSMENT

During the time students would normally complete Comprehension and Skill Activities, students will be administered a Written Assessment that can be found on page 105 in the students' *Activity Book 4*.

Note: See Making Decisions for additional assessment information.

12-DAY PLAN

Day 1

Teacher-Directed
- Exercise 1
- Story Opener: Judy Moody Saves the World
- Vocabulary, Ch. 1
- Judy Moody Saves the World, Ch. 1, pages 1–7
- Guide practice, as needed, on Dear Judy Moody Entries 1a, 1b and Comp & Skill 1

Independent Work
- On Your Own: Partner or Whisper Read, Judy Moody Saves the World, Ch. 1, pages 8–14
- Dear Judy Moody Entries 1a, 1b, Comp & Skill 1

Homework
- Homework Passage 1

Day 2

Teacher-Directed
- Exercise 2
- Vocabulary, Ch. 2
- Judy Moody Saves the World, Ch. 2, pages 15–19
- Guide practice, as needed, on Comp & Skill 2 and Dear Judy Moody Entries 2a, 2b

Independent Work
- On Your Own: Partner or Whisper Read, Judy Moody Saves the World, Ch. 2, pages 20–25
- Comp & Skill 2, Dear Judy Moody Entries 2a, 2b

Homework
- Homework Passage 2

Day 3

Teacher-Directed
- Exercise 3
- Vocabulary, Ch. 3
- Judy Moody Saves the World, Ch. 3, pages 26–33
- Guide practice, as needed, on Comp & Skill 3 and Dear Judy Moody Entries 3a, 3b

Independent Work
- On Your Own: Partner or Whisper Read, Judy Moody Saves the World, Ch. 3, pages 34–41
- Comp & Skill 3, Dear Judy Moody Entries 3a, 3b

Homework
- Homework Passage 3

Day 4

Teacher-Directed
- Exercise 4
- Vocabulary, Ch. 4
- Judy Moody Saves the World, Ch. 4, pages 42–48
- Guide practice, as needed, on Comp & Skill 4 and Dear Judy Moody Entries 4a, 4b

Independent Work
- On Your Own: Partner or Whisper Read, Judy Moody Saves the World, Ch. 4, pages 48–54
- Comp & Skill 4, Dear Judy Moody Entries 4a, 4b

Homework
- Homework Passage 4

Day 5

Teacher-Directed
- Exercise 5
- Vocabulary, Ch. 5, 6
- Judy Moody Saves the World, Ch. 5, pages 55–63
- Guide practice, as needed, on Comp & Skill 5 and Dear Judy Moody Entries 5a, 5b

Independent Work
- Repeated Reading: Partner or Whisper Read, Judy Moody Saves the World, Ch. 5, pages 55–63
- Comp & Skill 5, Dear Judy Moody Entries 5a, 5b

Homework
- Homework Passage 5

Day 6

Teacher-Directed
- Exercise 6
- Judy Moody Saves the World, Ch. 6, pages 64–71
- Guide practice, as needed, on Comp & Skill 6 and Dear Judy Moody Entries 6a, 6b

Independent Work
- On Your Own: Partner or Whisper Read, Judy Moody Saves the World, Ch. 6, pages 71–77
- Comp & Skill 6, Dear Judy Moody Entries 6a, 6b

Homework
- Homework Passage 6

Day 7

Teacher-Directed
- Exercise 7
- Vocabulary, Ch. 7
- Judy Moody Saves the World, Ch. 7, pages 78–84
- Guide practice, as needed, on Comp & Skill 7 and Dear Judy Moody Entries 7a, 7b

Independent Work
- On Your Own: Partner or Whisper Read, Judy Moody Saves the World, Ch. 7, pages 84–94
- Comp & Skill 7, Dear Judy Moody Entries 7a, 7b

Homework
- Homework Passage 7

Day 8

Teacher-Directed
- Exercise 8
- Vocabulary, Ch. 8
- Judy Moody Saves the World, Ch. 8, pages 95–100
- Guide practice, as needed, on Comp & Skill 8 and Dear Judy Moody Entries 8a, 8b

Independent Work
- On Your Own: Partner or Whisper Read, Judy Moody Saves the World, Ch. 8, pages 101–106
- Comp & Skill 8, Dear Judy Moody Entries 8a, 8b

Homework
- Homework Passage 8

Day 9	**Day 10**	**Day 11**	**Day 12**
Teacher-Directed • Exercise 9 • Vocabulary, Ch. 9, 10 • Judy Moody Saves the World, Ch. 9, pages 107–113 • Guide practice, as needed, on Comp & Skill 9 and Dear Judy Moody Entries 9a, 9b	**Teacher-Directed** • Exercise 10 • Judy Moody Saves the World, Ch. 10, pages 122–127 • Guide practice, as needed, on Comp & Skill 10, 11 and Dear Judy Moody Entries 10a, 10b	**Teacher-Directed** • Exercise 11 • Vocabulary, Ch. 11 • Judy Moody Saves the World, Ch. 11, pages 128–137 • Guide practice, as needed, on Comp & Skill 12 and Dear Judy Moody Entries 11a, 11b	**Teacher-Directed** • Exercise 12 • Fluency, Who Am I? **Independent Work** • Repeated Reading: Partner or Whisper Read, Who Am I? • Written Assessment • Oral Reading Fluency Assessment*
Independent Work • On Your Own: Partner or Whisper Read, Judy Moody Saves the World, Ch. 9, pages 114–121 • Comp & Skill 9, Dear Judy Moody Entries 9a, 9b	**Independent Work** • Repeated Reading: Partner or Whisper Read, Judy Moody Saves the World, Ch. 10, pages 122–127 • Comp & Skill 10, 11, Dear Judy Moody Entries 10a, 10b	**Independent Work** • On Your Own: Partner or Whisper Read, Judy Moody Saves the World, Ch. 11, pages 138–144 • Comp & Skill 12, Dear Judy Moody Entries 11a, 11b	**Homework** • Homework Passage 12
Homework • Homework Passage 9	**Homework** • Homework Passage 10	**Homework** • Homework Passage 11	

* The Oral Reading Fluency Assessments are individually administered by the teacher while students are working on their Written Assessments.

Materials and Materials Preparation

Core Lessons

Teacher Materials

READ WELL 2 MATERIALS

- Unit 24 Teacher's Guide
- Sound Cards
- Unit 24 Oral Reading Fluency Assessment found on page 148
- Group Assessment Record found in the *Assessment Manual*

SCHOOL SUPPLIES

Stopwatch or watch with a second hand

Student Materials

READ WELL 2 MATERIALS (for each student)

- *Judy Moody Saves the World*
- *Exercise Book 4*
- *Activity Book 4* or copies of Unit 24 Comprehension and Skill Work
- Unit 24 Written Assessment found in *Activity Book 4*, page 105, and on the blackline master CD
- Unit 24 Certificate of Achievement (BLM, page 149)
- Unit 24 Homework (blackline masters)
  See *Getting Started* for suggested homework routines.

SCHOOL SUPPLIES

Pencils, colors (optional—markers, crayons, or colored pencils)

Make one copy per student of each blackline master, as appropriate for the group.

Note: For new or difficult Comprehension and Skill Activities, make overhead transparencies from the blackline masters. Use the transparencies to demonstrate and guide practice.

SPECIAL NOTE

Your students will complete a Dear Judy Moody book. For ease of use, pull pages 47–58 from *Activity Book 4*. Staple the pages together into a book.

Important Tips

A Letter to the Kids
From the *Read Well* Authors

A LETTER TO THE KIDS FROM THE READ WELL AUTHORS

Dear Kids:

What a year! We had a grand time writing *Read Well 2*, and we hope you've had a grand time this year reading and learning with *Read Well 2*.

Oh my! You are such accomplished readers. You've read fiction and nonfiction. You've read books with great characters like Miss Tam, a detective dog, and a pufferfish named Pete. You've traveled to the Great Barrier Reef, the rain forest, and even Antarctica. You've read popular trade books— *Arthur's Pet Business, Dinosaurs Before Dark, Flat Stanley,* a *Magic School Bus* book, and even a Time for Kids book about Thomas Edison. What's next? Well, a Judy Moody book and an A to Z Mystery. Oh, and of course, you can have fun reading just about any book in the library.

We hope you will have time to cast your vote for your favorite character in the *Read Well* Literary Awards at the end of Unit 25. We also hope you'll write to us and tell us:

   —what your favorite story is and why.

   —what you think about your reading.

   —what you'd like to read about next.

   —the results of your awards.

We'll write you back! Hope to hear from you soon.

Send student letters to: *Read Well* Authors, P.O. Box 50550, Eugene, OR 97405. If you wish to receive a return note, include a postage paid, self-addressed envelope and a short description of your students (grade level and demographics). We would love to hear from you as well.

How to Teach the Lessons

Teach from this section. Each instructional component is outlined in an easy-to-teach format.

Exercise 1
- Story Opener: Judy Moody Saves the World!
- Vocabulary
- Story Reading 1
  With the Teacher: Chapter 1, Pages 1–7
  On Your Own: Chapter 1, Pages 8–14
- Dear Judy Moody Entries 1a, 1b, Comprehension and Skill Activity 1

Exercise 2
- Vocabulary
- Story Reading 2
  With the Teacher: Chapter 2, Pages 15–19
  On Your Own: Chapter 2, Pages 20–25
- Comprehension and Skill Activity 2, Dear Judy Moody Entries 2a, 2b

Exercise 3
- Vocabulary
- Story Reading 3
  With the Teacher: Chapter 3, Pages 26–33
  On Your Own: Chapter 3, Pages 34–41
- Comprehension and Skill Activity 3, Dear Judy Moody Entries 3a, 3b

Exercise 4
- Vocabulary
- Story Reading 4
  With the Teacher: Chapter 4, Pages 42–48
  On Your Own: Chapter 4, Pages 48–54
- Comprehension and Skill Activity 4, Dear Judy Moody Entries 4a, 4b

Exercise 5
- Vocabulary
- Story Reading 5
  With the Teacher: Chapter 5, Pages 55–63
- Comprehension and Skill Activity 5, Dear Judy Moody Entries 5a, 5b

Exercise 6
- Story Reading 6
  With the Teacher: Chapter 6, Pages 64–71
  On Your Own: Chapter 6, Pages 71–77
- Comprehension and Skill Activity 6, Dear Judy Moody Entries 6a, 6b

Note: Lessons include daily homework.

Exercise 7

- Vocabulary
- Story Reading 7
  With the Teacher: Chapter 7, Pages 78–84
  On Your Own: Chapter 7, Pages 84–94
- Comprehension and Skill Activity 7, Dear Judy Moody
  Entries 7a, 7b

Exercise 8

- Vocabulary
- Story Reading 8
  With the Teacher: Chapter 8, Pages 95–100
  On Your Own: Chapter 8, Pages 101–106
- Comprehension and Skill Activity 8, Dear Judy Moody
  Entries 8a, 8b

Exercise 9

- Vocabulary
- Story Reading 9
  With the Teacher: Chapter 9, Pages 107–113
  On Your Own: Chapter 9, Pages 114–121
- Comprehension and Skill Activity 9, Dear Judy Moody
  Entries 9a, 9b

Exercise 10

- Story Reading 10
  With the Teacher: Chapter 10, Pages 122–127
- Comprehension and Skill Activities 10, 11, Dear Judy
  Moody Entries 10a, 10b

Exercise 11

- Vocabulary
- Story Reading 11
  With the Teacher: Chapter 6, Pages 128–137
  On Your Own: Chapter 6, Pages 138–144
- Comprehension and Skill Activity 12, Dear Judy Moody Entries 11a, 11b

Exercise 12

- Story Reading 12
  With the Teacher: Who Am I? (Fluency)
- Written Assessment

Note: Lessons include daily homework.

❶ SHIFTY WORDS

❷ ACCURACY AND FLUENCY BUILDING

- For each task, have students say any underlined part, then read the word.
- Set a pace. Then have students read the whole words in each task and column.
- Provide repeated practice, building accuracy first, then fluency.

B2. Contractions

- Prompt students to tell you what a contraction is.
- Have students read the words, then the contraction.

C1. Multisyllabic Words

- For the list of words divided by syllables, have students read each syllable, then the whole word. Use the word in a sentence, as appropriate.
- For the list of whole words, build accuracy and then fluency.

universe	The Earth is a very, very small part of the entire . . . *universe.*
anaconda	A huge snake that lives in the rain forest is the . . . *anaconda.*
participants	Five people entered the race. There were five . . . *participants.*
pastels	My brother loves to draw with . . . *pastels.*
outrageous	Todd's story was unbelievable. It was . . . *outrageous.*
garbologist	Someone who studied garbage would be a . . . *garbologist.*
mascot	Janie's high school has a tiger for a . . . *mascot.*
fanatic	Geoffrey is really crazy about baseball. He is a baseball . . . *fanatic.*

D1. Tricky Words

- For each Tricky Word, have students use the sounds and word parts they know to silently sound out the word. Use the word in a sentence to help with pronunciation.
- If the word is unfamiliar, tell students the word.

annual

Look at the first word. The word is *annual.* Say the word. (annual) Annual means once a year. Every year we have a company picnic. We have an . . . *annual* . . . picnic.
Read the word three times. (annual, annual, annual)

receive	I got a game for my birthday. What did you . . . *receive?*
ecosystem	The rain forest has its own . . . *ecosystem.*
genius	Thomas Edison was a . . . *genius.*

- Have students go back and read the whole words in the column.

❸ WORDS IN CONTEXT

For each word, have students use the sounds and word parts they know to silently sound out the word. Then have students read the sentence. Assist, as needed.

❹ WORD ENDINGS

❺ NAMES, PLACES, AND ANIMALS

- Tell students these are people, places, and animals they will be reading about in the story.
- Have students use the sounds and word parts they know to figure out the words. Use the words in sentences, as needed.

PACING

Exercise 1 should take about 15 minutes.

SHIFTY WORDS CORRECTION PROCEDURE

If students make an error, put the word on the board. Underline the incorrect sound.

Have students identify the difficult sound, then sound the word out smoothly. Have students read the row again. Return to the difficult word for three correct responses.

⑥ GENERALIZATION: READING NEW WORDS IN PARAGRAPHS

- Have students read the paragraph silently, then out loud. Tell students to use the sounds and word parts they know to read any difficult words.
- Repeat practice, as needed.

Judy Moody Saves the World!

Unit 24 Exercise 1
Use before Chapter 1

1. SHIFTY WORDS Have students read the words.

slung	sling	sting	stink	blink

2. ACCURACY/FLUENCY BUILDING For each column, have students say any underlined part, then read each word. Next, have them read the column.

A1 Mixed Practice	**B1** Compound Words	**C1** Multisyllabic Words		**D1** Tricky Words
fr<u>ea</u>k	mailbox	u·ni·verse	universe	annual
t<u>oi</u>let	Band-Aid	an·a·con·da	anaconda	receive
elb<u>ow</u>s	rollerblades	par·ti·ci·pants	participants	ecosystem
band<u>age</u>	goldfish	pas·tels	pastels	genius
crank<u>y</u>	**B2** Contractions	out·ra·<u>geous</u>	outrageous	**D2** Reading by Analogy
f<u>o</u>nd	come on	gar·bol·o·gist	garbologist	pure
r<u>a</u>re	c'mon	mas·cot	mascot	figure
ank<u>le</u>s		fa·nat·ic	fanatic	cure

3. WORDS IN CONTEXT Have students use the sounds they know and then the sentences to pronounce each underlined word.

Ⓐ	crys·tal	Frank got a <u>crystal</u>-growing kit for his birthday.
Ⓑ	old-fash·ioned	Heather buys <u>old-fashioned</u> clothes at the used clothing store.

4. WORD ENDINGS Have students read the word, then the word with an ending.

<u>entering</u>	<u>squeaking</u>	<u>marker</u>	<u>reflexes</u>	<u>pencils</u>

5. NAMES, PLACES, AND ANIMALS Have students use the sounds and word parts they know to figure out the words.

Ⓐ	Judy Moody	Shenandoah salamander	monkeyface mussel
Ⓑ	cassowary	Picasso	Virginia

6. GENERALIZATION Have students read the paragraph silently, then out loud. (New words: Blackwell, design, mention, certificate, theme)

Ms. Blackwell entered a contest to design the new sign for the recycling building. She didn't win, but she did receive an Honorable Mention certificate. Her drawing was very creative. The theme for her design was reduce and reuse.

36

TEAM EXPECTATIONS

Acknowledge Team Efforts (Reminder)

Pair your compliments with team expectations. Say something like:
[Colton], I like the way you followed directions.

[Serena], you are sitting up so I can hear your great reading.

BUILD ACCURACY AND FLUENCY (Reminder)

For all rows and columns, follow the specific directions, then build accuracy and fluency with whole words.

GENERALIZATION (Reminder)

The generalization task provides an opportunity for you to informally assess students' ability to read new words that have not been pretaught.

COMPREHENSION PROCESSES
Remember, Understand, Apply

PROCEDURES

1. Introducing the Storybook

Viewing; Identifying—Title, Author, Illustrator; Inferring; Using Vocabulary—popular

Have students identify the title of their new storybook. Say something like:

Look at the cover. What's the title of the book? (Judy Moody Saves the World!)

Who's the author? (Megan McDonald)
Who's the illustrator? (Peter H. Reynolds)

Megan McDonald and Peter Reynolds have teamed up to write several books about Judy Moody. There are a lot of these books, so what do you know about them?
(They are popular.)

That's right. So they must be good!

2. Using the Table of Contents

Using Table of Contents; Identifying—Title; Predicting

Have students look at the Table of Contents. Say something like:

Turn to the Table of Contents.
Read the first four chapter titles.
(Crazy Strips Contest; Batty for Banana Peels; A Mr. Rubbish Mood; Pigtoes, Pumas, and Pimplebacks)

What can you tell about the book by the chapter titles? (It's going to be fun. It's going to be goofy . . .)

No. 3

Judy Moody
Saves
the
World!

Megan McDonald   illustrated by Peter H. Reynolds

1

> **MANAGEMENT TIP**
>
> For ease of reference, you may wish to number the book chapters on your copy of the table of contents.

Table of Contents

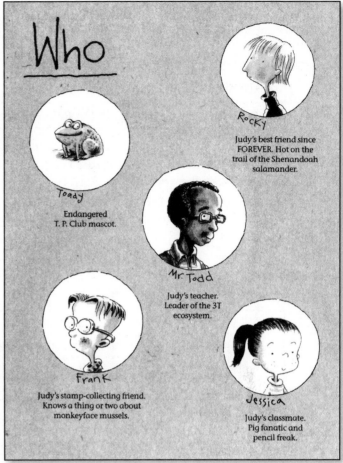

3. Using the Who's Who

Using the Who's Who; Identifying—Who; Inferring

Have students look at the Who's Who pages. Say something like:
Turn to the next pages. This book is great. It has a Who's Who. These pages
tell you a little about the characters in the book.

Find Judy Moody. Read the caption under Judy's picture.
(The heroine and garbologist, famous for her many moods.)

Does anyone know what a heroine is?
(It's like a girl hero.)

That's right! A heroine is a girl. She's usually a good or brave character in
a book.

The caption also says Judy is a garbologist. I've never heard of a garbologist
before. I think Megan McDonald made up that word.
What do you think a garbologist must do? (A garbologist must do something
with garbage.)
Yes, a garbologist must study garbage.

These are fun pages. We can use the Who's Who pages to find out about
the characters.

Now turn to page 1 of the story.

COMPREHENSION PROCESSES

Understand, Apply

PROCEDURES

Introducing Vocabulary

★reflex ★batty ★theme ★outrageous ★mood ★moody ★inspiration

- For each vocabulary word, have students read the word by parts, then read the whole word.
- Read the student-friendly explanations to students as they follow with their fingers. Then have students use the vocabulary word by following the gray text.
- Review and discuss the illustrations.

  Note: Student vocabulary pages for this unit are found in the students' *Exercise Book 4*.

USING VOCABULARY

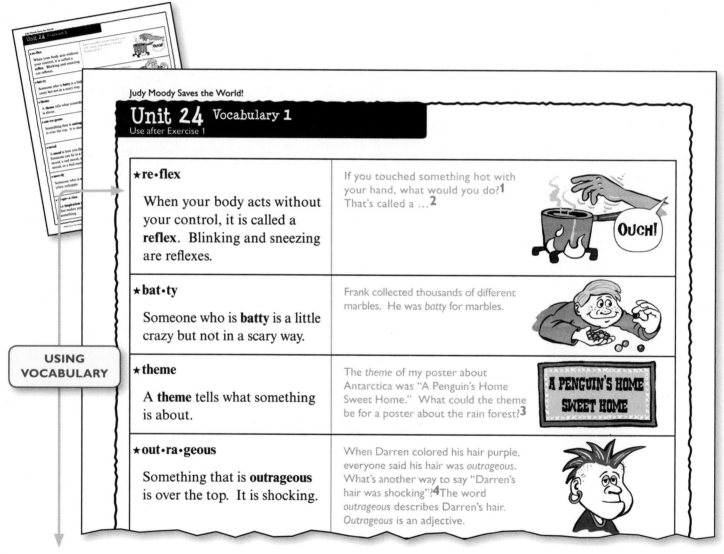

Judy Moody Saves the World!

Unit 24 Vocabulary **1**
Use after Exercise 1

★**re·flex**	If you touched something hot with your hand, what would you do?[1] That's called a …[2]
When your body acts without your control, it is called a **reflex**. Blinking and sneezing are reflexes.	
★**bat·ty**	Frank collected thousands of different marbles. He was *batty* for marbles.
Someone who is **batty** is a little crazy but not in a scary way.	
★**theme**	The *theme* of my poster about Antarctica was "A Penguin's Home Sweet Home." What could the theme be for a poster about the rain forest?[3]
A **theme** tells what something is about.	A PENGUIN'S HOME SWEET HOME
★**out·ra·geous**	When Darren colored his hair purple, everyone said his hair was *outrageous*. What's another way to say "Darren's hair was shocking"?[4] The word *outrageous* describes Darren's hair. *Outrageous* is an adjective.
Something that is **outrageous** is over the top. It is shocking.	

❶ **Understand:** Using Vocabulary—reflex (I would pull my hand away.)

❷ **Understand:** Using Vocabulary—reflex (reflex)

❸ **Apply:** Using Vocabulary—theme, protect (The theme for a poster about the rain forest could be "Protecting the Environment.")

❹ **Apply:** Using Vocabulary—outrageous (Darren's hair was outrageous.)

★ = New in this unit

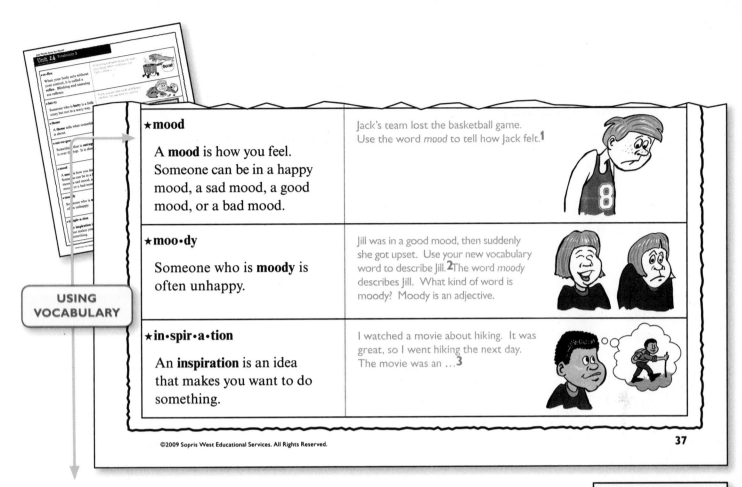

★**mood**	Jack's team lost the basketball game. Use the word *mood* to tell how Jack felt.[1]
A **mood** is how you feel. Someone can be in a happy mood, a sad mood, a good mood, or a bad mood.	
★**moo·dy**	Jill was in a good mood, then suddenly she got upset. Use your new vocabulary word to describe Jill.[2] The word *moody* describes Jill. What kind of word is moody? Moody is an adjective.
Someone who is **moody** is often unhappy.	
★**in·spir·a·tion**	I watched a movie about hiking. It was great, so I went hiking the next day. The movie was an …[3]
An **inspiration** is an idea that makes you want to do something.	

37

USING VOCABULARY

❶ **Understand:** Using Vocabulary—mood (Jack was in a sad mood.)

❷ **Understand:** Defining and Using Vocabulary—moody (Jill was moody.)

❸ **Apply:** Using Vocabulary—inspiration (inspiration)

> **USING VOCABULARY**
>
> Be enthusiastic about learning new words. Keep a running list of words you would like to use and encourage students to use. Keep the list handy when you are teaching. Put students' names on the board to acknowledge use of a word. Say things like:
> Wow! [Rod] used the word *inspiration* when he talked about his idea for a painting. That's a great way to use a vocabulary word!

STORY READING INSTRUCTIONS

Students read Chapter 1 (Crazy Strips Contest), pages 1–7 with the teacher and pages 8–14 on their own.

COMPREHENSION PROCESSES

Remember, Understand, Apply, Analyze

COMPREHENSION BUILDING

• Encourage students to answer questions with complete sentences.
• If students have difficulty comprehending, think aloud with them or reread the portion of the story that answers the question. Repeat the question.

PROCEDURES

1. Introducing Chapter 1 (Crazy Strips Contest)

Identifying—Title; Inferring

Have students read the title. Say something like:

Turn to page 1. Read the title of the chapter. (Crazy Strips Contest)

Why do you think the author named the chapter "Crazy Strips Contest"?

2. First Reading

• Ask questions and discuss the story as indicated by the blue text in this guide.
• Mix group and individual turns, independent of your voice.
  Have students work toward a group accuracy goal of 0–6 errors.
  Quietly keep track of errors made by all students in the group.
• After reading the story, practice any difficult words.
  Reread the story if students have not reached the accuracy goal.

3. Second Reading, Short Passage Practice: Developing Prosody

• Demonstrate expressive, fluent reading of the first two paragraphs.
• Guide practice with your voice.
• Provide individual turns while others track with their fingers and whisper read.
• Repeat with one paragraph at a time.

> **CORRECTING DECODING ERRORS**
>
> During story reading, gently correct any error, then have students reread the sentence.

> **REPEATED READINGS**
>
> **Prosody**
>
> On the second reading, students practice developing prosody—phrasing and expression. Research has shown that prosody is related to both fluency and comprehension.

Crazy Strips Contest

Judy Moody did not set out to save the world. She set out to win a contest. A Band-Aid contest.

Judy snapped open her doctor kit. Where was that box of Crazy Strips? She lifted out the tiny hammer for testing reflexes.

"Hey, can I try that?" asked Stink, coming into Judy's room.

"Stink, didn't you ever hear of going knock, knock?"

PG 1

After Reading the Chapter Title

❶ Apply: Inferring
What is this chapter about?
(It's about a contest.)

❷ Apply: Inferring—Goal
Crazy strips are bandages. What do you think will be Judy Moody's goal in this chapter?
(She wants to win a contest.)
After we read the first paragraph, let's write Judy Moody's goal on the board so we can keep it in mind as we read.

After Reading Page 1

❶ Apply: Inferring
The story doesn't tell us, but we can figure it out. Who is Stink? (Stink is Judy's brother.)

❷ Apply: Inferring, Explaining
What did Judy want Stink to do before he went into her room?
(She wanted him to knock on her door.)

❸ Understand: Identifying—What
What did Stink want to try out?
(Stink wanted to try the little hammer in Judy's doctor kit.)

PG 3

After Reading Page 2 and Viewing Page 3

❶ **Apply:** Inferring; Using Vocabulary—reflex
Look at the picture. When Judy hit Stink's knee with the little hammer, what was she testing?
(She was testing his reflexes.)

❷ **Apply:** Inferring; Explaining; Using Vocabulary—reflex
Why did Stink kick Judy?
(She tested his reflexes, and they worked.)

After Reading Page 4

❶ **Remember:** Identifying—What
What is a cassowary?
(A cassowary is a rain forest bird.)

❷ **Apply:** Inferring, Explaining
Why did Judy ask Stink if he was a cassowary?
(Stink kicked Judy. That's what a cassowary does to its enemies.)

After Reading Page 5

❶ **Understand:** Explaining
What did the kids need to do to enter the Crazy Strips contest?
(They had to design a bandage.)

❷ **Remember:** Identifying—What
What did Stink ask about the contest?
(He asked, "What do we win?")

After Reading Page 6

❶ **Apply:** Inferring, Explaining
Why was Judy excited about the possibility of
winning the Crazy Strip Contest?
(If she won, everyone would be wearing her
design. She thought it might make her famous.)

After Reading Page 7

❶ **Apply:** Inferring, Explaining
Why did Stink want to win the Crazy
Strip Contest?
(He wanted to win the rollerblades.)

❷ **Analyze:** Drawing Conclusions
Do you think Stink cared about being famous?
(No, he just wanted new skates . . .)

STORY READING INSTRUCTIONS

Students read pages 8–14 without the teacher, independently or with partners.

COMPREHENSION PROCESSES

Remember, Understand, Apply, Create

PROCEDURES FOR READING ON YOUR OWN

1. Getting Ready

Have students turn to page 8.

2. Setting a Purpose

Generating Ideas; Identifying—How; Describing; Explaining; Using Vocabulary—mood

Before students begin reading, say something like:

Now you'll finish the chapter on your own. We'll read to learn more about what Judy and Stink do to enter the contest. Some questions for you to think about as you read are on the board.

- If you were Stink or Judy, what might you draw for a Crazy Strip design?
- How did Judy try to discourage Stink?
- Describe Stink's design and message.
- Why did Judy end up in a bad mood?

> **PREP NOTE**
> **Setting a Purpose**
> Write questions on a chalkboard, white board, or large piece of paper before working with your small group.

3. Reading on Your Own: Partner or Whisper Reading

- Have students take turns reading every other page with a partner or have students whisper read pages 8–14 on their own.
- Continue having students track each word with their fingers.

4. Comprehension and Skill Work

Tell students that after they read on their own, they will draw a picture of Judy Moody's mood at the end of the chapter and write a letter to Judy Moody. They will also do Comprehension and Skill Activity 1. Guide practice, as needed. For teacher directions, see pages 25–27.

5. Homework 1: New Passage

ENTRIES 1a, 1b

COMPREHENSION PROCESSES

Understand, Evaluate, Create

WRITING TRAITS

Ideas and Content
Word Choice
Conventions—Complete Sentence,
Capital, Period
Presentation

Following Directions
Sentence Completion

Unit 24 Dear Judy Moody   Use after Exercise 1 and Chapter 1

Dear Judy Moody
Letters and Notes for Your Not-So-Moody Friend

Ana Lopez

The Many Faces of Judy Moody	Entry 1b Crazy Strips Contest	Entry 2b Batty for Banana Peels	Entry 3b A Mr. Rubbish Mood
Entry 11b The Winking Disease	Mood Chart		Entry 4b Pigtoes, Pumas, and Pimplebacks
Entry 10b Batty for Bottles			Entry 5b Beetle Emergency
Entry 9b Project P.E.N.C.I.L.	Entry 8b Batty for Band-Aids	Entry 7b Luna Two	Entry 6b Pond Scum

Mood Chart: happy, moody, proud, jealous, worried, upset, excited, angry

Teachers: If you are using the Activity Book, tear out and staple pages 47–58 to make a separate Book Journal.

> **SPECIAL NOTE**
> Your students will complete a Dear Judy Moody book. For ease of use, pull pages 47–58 out of *Activity Book 4*. Staple the pages together into a book.

PROCEDURES

Have students complete the page independently. Guide practice, only as needed.

1. **Dear Judy Moody—Introductory Instructions**
   Have students write their name on the cover as the author of the letters to Judy Moody.

2. **Letter Writing: Creative Writing—Specific Instructions** (Entry 1a)
   • Tell students to turn to the next page. Have them fill in the blanks to complete a letter to Judy Moody. Encourage them to use snazzy vocabulary words.
   • Remind students to start sentences with a capital and end with a period.
   • After they complete their letter, have them read and follow the directions at the bottom of the page.

3. **Cover: Illustrating—Specific Instructions** (Entry 1b)
   • Have students look at the feelings chart, then read and discuss the different moods.
   • Have students find the box on page 25 labeled Entry 1b and draw a face that shows Judy's mood at the end of the chapter they just finished.

ENTRIES 1a, 1b

Following Directions
Generating Ideas, Responding
Sentence Completion

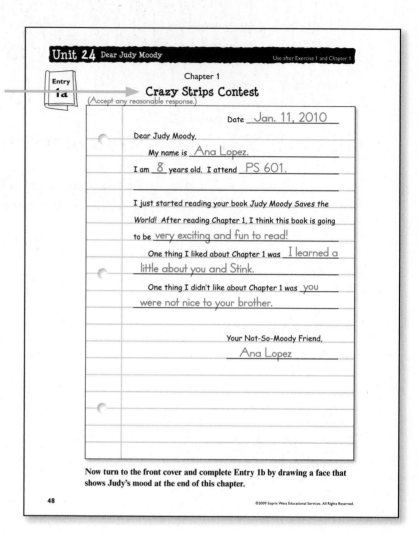

Unit 24 Dear Judy Moody — Use after Exercise 1 and Chapter 1

Entry
1a

Chapter 1

Crazy Strips Contest
(Accept any reasonable response.)

Date _Jan. 11, 2010_

Dear Judy Moody,

My name is _Ana Lopez._

I am _8_ years old. I attend _PS 601._

I just started reading your book *Judy Moody Saves the World!* After reading Chapter 1, I think this book is going to be _very exciting and fun to read!_

One thing I liked about Chapter 1 was _I learned a little about you and Stink._

One thing I didn't like about Chapter 1 was _you were not nice to your brother._

Your Not-So-Moody Friend,
Ana Lopez

Now turn to the front cover and complete Entry 1b by drawing a face that shows Judy's mood at the end of this chapter.

48

©2009 Sopris West Educational Services. All Rights Reserved.

STORY COMPREHENSION

COMPREHENSION PROCESSES
Remember, Understand, Analyze

WRITING TRAITS
Conventions—Complete Sentence, Capital, Period
Presentation

Identifying—Main Character, Character Traits (Characterization)

Identifying—What

Identifying—What; Illustrating

Using Graphic Organizer; Explaining Sentence Completion

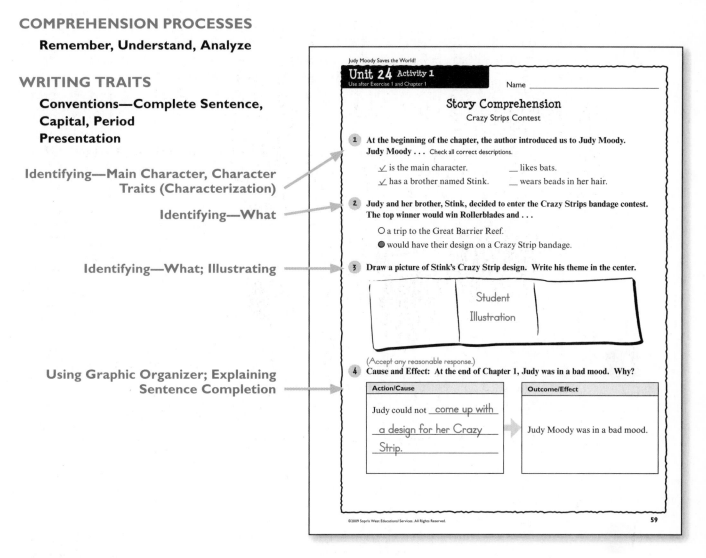

Judy Moody Saves the World!

Unit 24 Activity 1
Use after Exercise 1 and Chapter 1

Name _____

Story Comprehension
Crazy Strips Contest

1. At the beginning of the chapter, the author introduced us to Judy Moody. Judy Moody . . . Check all correct descriptions.

   ✓ is the main character.   __ likes bats.
   ✓ has a brother named Stink.   __ wears beads in her hair.

2. Judy and her brother, Stink, decided to enter the Crazy Strips bandage contest. The top winner would win Rollerblades and . . .

   ○ a trip to the Great Barrier Reef.
   ● would have their design on a Crazy Strip bandage.

3. Draw a picture of Stink's Crazy Strip design. Write his theme in the center.

       Student Illustration

(Accept any reasonable response.)

4. Cause and Effect: At the end of Chapter 1, Judy was in a bad mood. Why?

Action/Cause		Outcome/Effect
Judy could not <u>come up with a design for her Crazy Strip.</u>	→	Judy Moody was in a bad mood.

59

PROCEDURES
For each step, demonstrate and guide practice, as needed. Then have students complete the page independently.

1. **Selection Response—Basic Instructions** (Items 1 and 2)
   Have students read the sentence starters, then check all descriptions that apply or fill in the bubble for the correct answer.

2. **Illustrating, Theme—Specific Instructions** (Item 3)
   Have students draw a picture of Stink's Crazy Strip design, then write his theme in the center of their drawing.

3. **Cause/Effect: Sequence Chart—Specific Instructions** (Item 4)
   Have students explain the outcome by completing the sentence in the box in the first column. Remind students to look back in their storybook, if needed.

Self-monitoring
Have students check and correct their work.

❶ SOUND REVIEW

❷ SOUND PRACTICE
- For each task, have students spell and say the focus sound in the gray bar.
- Next, have students read each underlined sound, the word, then the whole column.
- Repeat with each column, building accuracy first, then fluency.

❸ ACCURACY AND FLUENCY BUILDING

B1. Related Words

Tell students these words are related to the word "imagine." Have them read the words.

C1. Multisyllabic Words
- For the list of words divided by syllables, have students read each syllable, then the whole word. Use the word in a sentence, as appropriate.
- For the list of whole words, build accuracy and then fluency.

environment	The frogs couldn't live in a dry . . . *environment.*
cursive	When you write by joining letters together, you are writing in . . . *cursive.*
difference	Ellen wanted to contribute and make a . . . *difference.*
garbage	Something that we throw away is . . . *garbage.*
litterbugs	People who litter are . . . *litterbugs.*
jitterbugs	Jerold couldn't stop moving. He had the . . . *jitterbugs.*

> **ACCURACY AND FLUENCY BUILDING**
> **(Reminder)**
>
> For each task, have students say any underlined part, then read the word.
>
> Set a pace. Then have students read the whole words in each task and column.
>
> Provide repeated practice, building accuracy first, then fluency.

D1. Tricky Words
- For each Tricky Word, have students use the sounds and word parts they know to silently sound out the word. Use the word in a sentence to help with pronunciation.

double
Look at the first word. It rhymes with *trouble*. Read the word. (double)
Two times as many or twice as much of something is . . . *double.*
Read the word two times. (double, double)

pearl	For Christmas, Dad got Mom a . . . *pearl* . . . necklace.
fourth	Paco didn't come in first, second, or third. He came in . . . *fourth.*
borrow	Tonya wanted to use Ned's bike, so she asked to . . . *borrow* . . . it.
tomorrow	I could clean house today, but I think I'll do it . . . *tomorrow.*

- Have students go back and read the whole words in the column.

❹ WORD ENDINGS

❺ MORPHOGRAPHS AND AFFIXES
- Have students read the underlined part, then the whole word.
- Review the morphograph *bi-*, as time allows. Say something like:
  Put your finger on the next word. Read the underlined part, then the word. (bi, biannual)
  What does *bi-* mean? (two) Right. Annual is once a year. So *biannual* means . . . two times a year.

- Repeat practice with whole words, mixing group and individual turns.
  Build accuracy, then fluency.

6 **GENERALIZATION: READING NEW WORDS IN PARAGRAPHS**
- Have students read the paragraph silently, then out loud. Tell students to use the sounds and word parts they know to read any difficult words.
- Repeat practice, as needed.

Judy Moody Saves the World!

Unit 24 Exercise 2
Use before Chapter 2

1. SOUND REVIEW Use selected Sound Cards from Units 1–19.

2. SOUND PRACTICE In each column, have students spell and say the sound, next say any underlined sound and the word, then read the column.

ā	ou	ci, ce	ee, ea
cr<u>a</u>zy	<u>mou</u>se	<u>sci</u>ence	p<u>ee</u>l
p<u>a</u>per	b<u>ou</u>nce	pe<u>ace</u>	sh<u>ee</u>sh
t<u>a</u>ble	playgr<u>ou</u>nd	medi<u>ci</u>ne	h<u>ea</u>l

3. ACCURACY/FLUENCY BUILDING For each column, have students say any underlined part, then read each word. Next, have them read the column.

A1 Mixed Practice	B1 Related Words	C1 Multisyllabic Words		D1 Tricky Words
d<u>ea</u>d	imagine	en·vi·ron·ment	environment	double
sm<u>oo</u>sh	imagining	cur·sive	cursive	pearl
gl<u>o</u>be	imaginative	dif·fer·ence	difference	fourth
r<u>i</u>sk	imagination	gar·bage	garbage	borrow
c<u>a</u>rds		lit·ter·bugs	litterbugs	tomorrow
<u>kn</u>ocking		jit·ter·bugs	jitterbugs	

4. WORD ENDINGS Have students read each underlined word, then the word with an ending.

<u>compost</u>ing	<u>disappear</u>ing	<u>decay</u>ed	<u>litter</u>ing
replace replacing	health healthy		die dying

5. MORPHOGRAPHS AND AFFIXES Have students read each underlined part, then the word.

invis<u>ible</u>	un<u>less</u>	discus<u>sion</u>	<u>bi</u>annual	<u>in</u>stead

6. GENERALIZATION Have students read the paragraph silently, then out loud. (New words: Hailey, award-winning, finch)

Hailey wrote an award-winning play. The play is about a little bird called a finch. The director of the play thinks it's fantastic and Hailey's best work. Hailey's next play is going to be about a bird called a cassowary.

cassowary

finch

COMPREHENSION PROCESSES

Understand, Apply

PROCEDURES

Introducing Vocabulary

> creative ★ environment, recycle, composting ★ heal

- For each vocabulary word, have students read the word by parts, then read the whole word.
- Read the student-friendly explanations to students as they follow with their fingers. Then have students use the vocabulary word by following the gray text.
- Review and discuss the illustrations.
  Note: Student vocabulary pages for this unit are found in the students' *Exercise Book 4*.

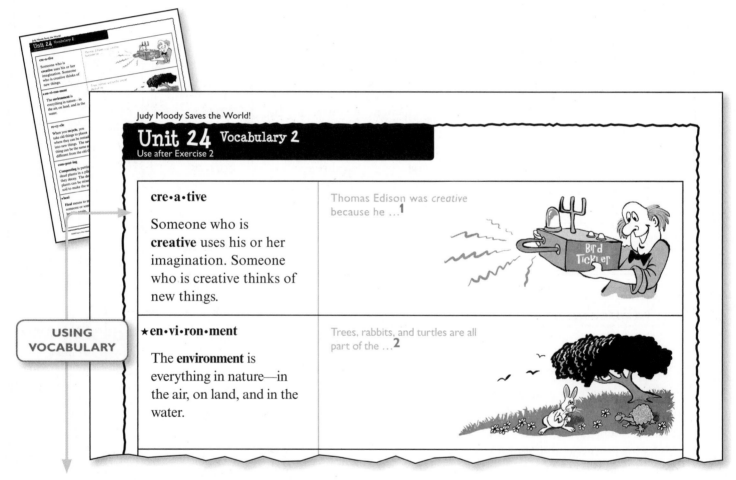

USING VOCABULARY

Judy Moody Saves the World!

Unit 24 Vocabulary 2
Use after Exercise 2

cre•a•tive

Someone who is **creative** uses his or her imagination. Someone who is creative thinks of new things.

Thomas Edison was *creative* because he …**1**

★en•vi•ron•ment

The **environment** is everything in nature—in the air, on land, and in the water.

Trees, rabbits, and turtles are all part of the …**2**

❶ **Apply:** Using Vocabulary—creative (invented many things)
❷ **Apply:** Using Vocabulary—environment (environment)

★ = New in this unit

USING VOCABULARY

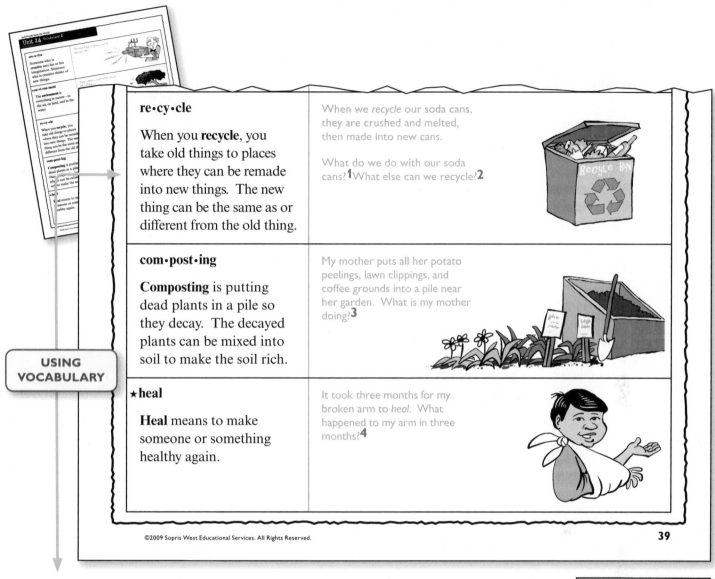

re·cy·cle

When you **recycle**, you take old things to places where they can be remade into new things. The new thing can be the same as or different from the old thing.

When we *recycle* our soda cans, they are crushed and melted, then made into new cans.

What do we do with our soda cans?**1** What else can we recycle?**2**

com·post·ing

Composting is putting dead plants in a pile so they decay. The decayed plants can be mixed into soil to make the soil rich.

My mother puts all her potato peelings, lawn clippings, and coffee grounds into a pile near her garden. What is my mother doing?**3**

★heal

Heal means to make someone or something healthy again.

It took three months for my broken arm to *heal*. What happened to my arm in three months?**4**

39

❶ **Apply:** Using Vocabulary—recycle (We recycle our soda cans.)

❷ **Apply:** Using Vocabulary—recycle (We can recycle newspapers, cardboard, glass, bottles, plastic containers . . .)

❸ **Apply:** Using Vocabulary—composting (My mother is composting.)

❹ **Understand:** Using Vocabulary—heal (The arm got healthy again.)

USING VOCABULARY

Be enthusiastic about learning new words. Keep a running list of words you would like to use and encourage students to use. Keep the list handy when you are teaching. Put students' names on the board to acknowledge use of a word. Say things like:

[Seth] used the word *environment* when he was talking about pollution. What a great way to use a sophisticated vocabulary word!

CHAPTER 2 INSTRUCTIONS

Students read Chapter 2 (Batty for Banana Peels), pages 15–19 with the teacher and pages 20–25 on their own.

COMPREHENSION PROCESSES

Remember, Understand, Apply, Evaluate, Create

PROCEDURES

1. **Reviewing Pages 8–14**

   Summarizing; Locating Information; Inferring—Goal; Making Connections; Describing; Inferring; Defining and/or Using Vocabulary—discourage, inspiration

   Discuss questions from the board.

   You read the last part of Chapter 1 on your own. Let's talk about what you learned.

   If we can't remember, what can we do? (We can look in our books.)

   What was Judy's goal in Chapter 1? (Her goal was to win the Crazy Strips contest.)

   If you were Stink or Judy, what might you draw for a Crazy Strip design?

   (I might draw trees or a picture of the Earth . . .)

   How did Judy try to discourage Stink? Let's go back to the top of page 8 and read what Judy told Stink. (Dream on, Stink . . .) So how did Judy try to discourage Stink?

   (She said only one person would win. She said the kids who won were older than Stink.)

   Describe Stink's design and message. (It had bats and said "Batty for Band-Aids" . . .)

   Why did Judy end up in a bad mood?

   (Stink sent his entry in before Judy even came up with an idea . . .)

   At the end of this chapter, Judy needs an inspiration. What is an inspiration?

   (An inspiration is an idea that makes you want to do something . . .)

2. **Introducing Chapter 2 (Batty for Banana Peels)**

   Using Table of Contents; Identifying—Title; Defining and Using Vocabulary—batty; Inferring; Predicting

   Discuss the title. Say something like:

   Find the Table of Contents. What's the title of the second chapter? (Batty for Banana Peels)

   Can you remember where we've seen the word *batty* before? Look back in your books, if you need to. Yes, Stink's theme for his Crazy Strip is "Batty for Band-Aids."

   What does *batty* mean? (It means you're crazy about something.)

   So what do you think this chapter will be about? (someone who really likes banana peels . . .)

3. **First Reading**

   • Ask questions and discuss the story as indicated by the blue text in this guide.
   • Mix group and individual turns, independent of your voice.
     Have students work toward a group accuracy goal of 0–5 errors.
   • After reading the story, practice any difficult words.
     Reread the story if students have not reached the accuracy goal.

4. **Second Reading, Timed Readings: Repeated Reading**

   • As time allows, have students do Timed Readings while others follow along.
   • Time individuals for 30 seconds.
   • Determine words correct per minute. Record student scores.

Batty for Banana Peels

All day Saturday and all day Sunday, Judy could not think up one single creative, award-winning Crazy Strips idea. On Monday morning, as soon as she got to the bus stop, Judy told her best friend, Rocky, about the contest. "Help me think of an idea!"

"I know," said Rocky. "How about a disappearing one? You put it on your arm, only it's clear, so it's invisible."

15

After Reading Page 15

❶ **Understand:** Identifying—Problem; Using Vocabulary—creative
What was Judy's problem?
(She couldn't think of a creative Crazy Strip idea.)

❷ **Remember:** Identifying—Who
Who is Rocky?
(Rocky is Judy's best friend.)

❸ **Remember:** Identifying—What
What was Rocky's idea for the Crazy Strip?
(His idea was a disappearing, or invisible, Crazy Strip.)

❹ **Evaluate:** Making Judgments; **Understand:** Explaining
Do you think Rocky's idea for the contest is a good idea? Why or why not?
(Yes, it would be cool. No, the judges couldn't see your design . . .)

After Reading Page 16

❶ **Understand:** Explaining
Why didn't Judy think Rocky's idea was a
good one?
(She wanted the world to see her design.)

After Reading Page 17

❶ **Understand:** Locating Information; Describing—
Character Traits (Characterization);
Who is Frank Pearl? How can we find out?
(We can look at the Who's Who in the front of
the book.)
Turn back to the Who's Who section.
What does it say about Frank?
(He is Judy's friend. He collects stamps.)

❷ **Understand:** Describing—Character Traits
(Characterization)
Who is Jessica?
(Jessica is Judy's classmate. It says she's a pig
fanatic and a pencil freak.)
That means Jessica loves pigs and pencils. She must
be an interesting girl!

After Reading Page 18

❶ **Apply:** Inferring—Who
Who is Mr. Todd?
(Mr. Todd is Judy's science teacher.)

❷ **Understand:** Summarizing;
Using Vocabulary—environment
What was Judy's class learning about in
science class?
(They were studying the environment and how to
help save the Earth.)

❸ **Understand:** Summarizing—Problems
Mr. Todd mentioned three problems with
the environment. What were they?
(Malls are replacing trees, animals are disappearing,
and we're running out of places to put our trash.)

After Reading Page 19

❶ **Understand:** Summarizing—Solutions; Using
Vocabulary—recycle, composting
What were some of the solutions the class came
up with to help the environment?
(Don't leave lights on, recycle stuff, start
composting, and plant trees.)

❷ **Apply:** Making Connections; Using Vocabulary—
recycle
Which of these things do you already do?
(We have a recycle bin. We planted a tree last
year . . .)

❸ **Create:** Generating Ideas
Can you think of other solutions that would help
save the Earth?
(Walk to school instead of having your mom drive
you. Wear a sweater and turn the heat down . . .)

STORY READING INSTRUCTIONS

Students read pages 20–25 without the teacher, independently or with partners.

COMPREHENSION PROCESSES

Remember, Understand, Apply, Create

PROCEDURES FOR READING ON YOUR OWN

1. Getting Ready

Have students turn to page 20.

2. Setting a Purpose

Identifying—Problem; Explaining; Predicting; Inferring

Before students begin reading, say something like:

Now you'll finish the chapter on your own. At the beginning of the chapter, what was Judy's problem?

(She needed an idea for the contest.)

Let's read to see if she can come up with an idea for the Crazy Strips contest. Some questions for you to think about as you read are on the board:

- Why did Judy want Rocky to eat bananas?
- What was Judy's idea for the Crazy Strip contest?
- What did Judy mean when she said, "There's going to be a few changes around here"?

> **PREP NOTE**
>
> **Setting a Purpose**
> Write questions on a chalkboard, white board, or large piece of paper before working with your small group.

3. Reading on Your Own: Partner or Whisper Reading

- Have students take turns reading every other page with a partner or have students whisper read pages 20–25 on their own.
- Continue having students track each word with their fingers.

4. Comprehension and Skill Work

Tell students that after they read on their own, they will do Comprehension and Skill Activity 2, write their second letter to Judy Moody, and then draw her mood on the cover. Guide practice, as needed. For teacher directions, see pages 37 and 38.

5. Homework 2: New Passage

STORY COMPREHENSION

COMPREHENSION PROCESSES

Remember, Understand, Apply

WRITING TRAITS

Conventions—Complete Sentence, Capital, Period
Presentation

Identifying—What

Summarizing

Identifying—How

Identifying—What; Illustrating

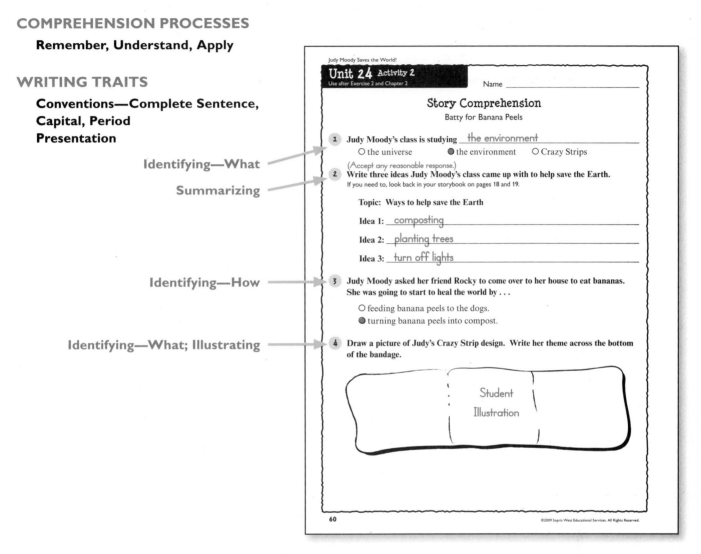

Judy Moody Saves the World!

Unit 24 Activity 2
Use after Exercise 2 and Chapter 2

Name _____

Story Comprehension
Batty for Banana Peels

1 Judy Moody's class is studying ___the environment___
  ○ the universe   ● the environment   ○ Crazy Strips
  (Accept any reasonable response.)

2 Write three ideas Judy Moody's class came up with to help save the Earth.
  If you need to, look back in your storybook on pages 18 and 19.

  Topic: Ways to help save the Earth

  Idea 1: ___composting___

  Idea 2: ___planting trees___

  Idea 3: ___turn off lights___

3 Judy Moody asked her friend Rocky to come over to her house to eat bananas. She was going to start to heal the world by . . .
  ○ feeding banana peels to the dogs.
  ● turning banana peels into compost.

4 Draw a picture of Judy's Crazy Strip design. Write her theme across the bottom of the bandage.

  Student
  Illustration

60

©2009 Sopris West Educational Services. All Rights Reserved.

PROCEDURES

For each step, demonstrate and guide practice, as needed. Then have students complete the page independently.

1. **Selection Response—Basic Instructions** (Items 1 and 3)
   Have students read the sentence starter, then fill in the bubble and/or write the correct answer in the blank.

2. **Making Lists: Locating Information—Specific Instructions** (Item 2)
   Have students read the directions, then list three ideas that Judy's class came up with to help save the Earth. Remind students to look back in Chapter 2.

3. **Illustrating, Theme—Specific Instructions** (Item 4)
   Have students draw a picture of Judy's Crazy Strip design, then write her theme across the bottom.

Self-monitoring

Have students check and correct their work.

ENTRIES 2a, 2b

COMPREHENSION PROCESSES
Understand, Evaluate, Create

WRITING TRAITS
Ideas and Content
Word Choice
Conventions—Complete Sentence, Capital, Period
Presentation

SPECIAL NOTE

Your students will complete a Dear Judy Moody book. For ease of use, pull pages 47–58 from *Activity Book 4*. Staple the pages together into a book.

PROCEDURES
Have students complete the page independently. Guide practice, only as needed.

Letter Writing: Creative Writing—Specific Instructions (Entry 2a)
Have students fill in the blanks to complete a letter to Judy Moody. Encourage them to use at least one of the snazzy vocabulary words listed in the box.
Remind them to start sentences with a capital and end with a period.

Cover: Illustrating—Specific Instructions (Entry 2b)
Have students find the box labeled Entry 2b on the cover and draw a face that shows Judy's mood at the end of this chapter. Remind them to look back in their book, if needed.

Generating Ideas
Responding
Sentence
Completion

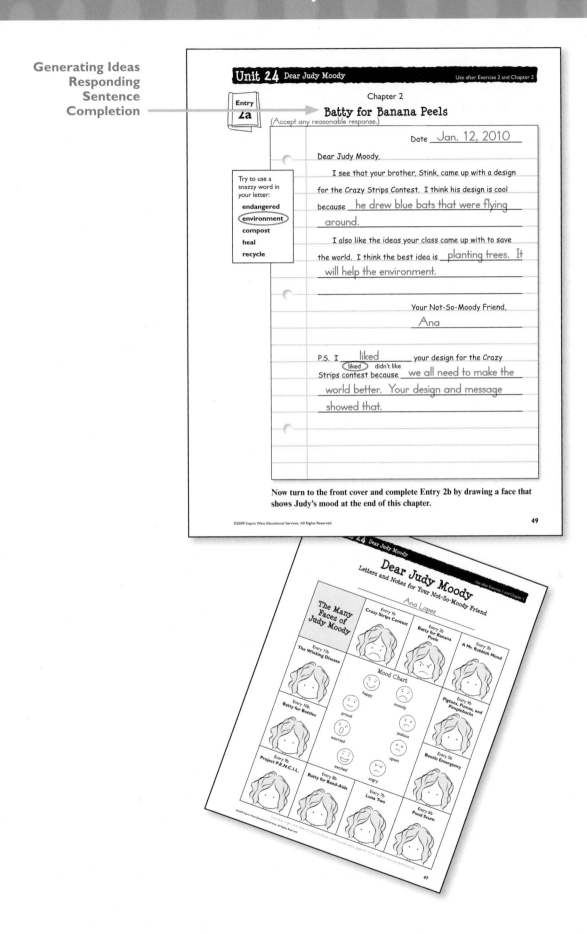

Unit 24 Dear Judy Moody   Use after Exercise 2 and Chapter 2

Entry 2a

Chapter 2

Batty for Banana Peels
(Accept any reasonable response.)

Date Jan. 12, 2010

Dear Judy Moody,

I see that your brother, Stink, came up with a design for the Crazy Strips Contest. I think his design is cool because he drew blue bats that were flying around.

I also like the ideas your class came up with to save the world. I think the best idea is planting trees. It will help the environment.

Your Not-So-Moody Friend,

Ana

P.S. I liked your design for the Crazy Strips contest because we all need to make the world better. Your design and message showed that.

Try to use a snazzy word in your letter:
endangered
environment
compost
heal
recycle

liked   didn't like

Now turn to the front cover and complete Entry 2b by drawing a face that shows Judy's mood at the end of this chapter.

©2009 Sopris West Educational Services. All Rights Reserved.   49

Dear Judy Moody
Letters and Notes for Your Not-So-Moody Friend

Ana Lopez

The Many Faces of Judy Moody

Entry 1b — Crazy Strips Contest
Entry 2b — Batty for Banana Peels
Entry 3b — A Mr. Rubbish Mood

Entry 11b — The Winking Disease

Mood Chart
happy
moody
proud
jealous
worried
excited
upset
angry

Entry 10b — Batty for Bottles

Entry 4b — Pigtoes, Pumas, and Pimplebacks

Entry 9b — Project P.E.N.C.I.L.

Entry 8b — Batty for Band-Aids

Entry 7b — Luna Two

Entry 5b — Beetle Emergency

Entry 6b — Pond Scum

47

❶ SOUND PRACTICE

- For each task, have students spell and say the focus sound in the gray bar. For Mixed Practice, read the header.
- Next, have students read each underlined sound, the word, then the whole column.
- Repeat with each column, building accuracy first, then fluency.

❷ ACCURACY AND FLUENCY BUILDING

- For each task, have students say any underlined part, then read the word.
- Set a pace. Then have students read the whole words in each task and column.
- Provide repeated practice, building accuracy first, then fluency.

B1. Compound Words

> Ask students what a compound word is.
> Then have them read the words.

C1. Multisyllabic Words

> Have students read each whole word.
> Use each word in a sentence, as needed.

E1. Tricky Words

- For each Tricky Word, have students use the sounds and word parts they know to silently sound out the word. Use the word in a sentence to help with pronunciation.

> MULTISYLLABIC WORDS CORRECTION PROCEDURE
>
> If students make an error, put the word on the board. Draw loops under each syllable and guide practice with your hand. Have students say each syllable then read the whole word.

oxygen	Trees take in carbon dioxide and give off . . . *oxygen.*
warming	I got in front of the fire and started . . . *warming . . .* my hands.
sorry	I accidentally broke my sister's bracelet, so I told her I was . . . *sorry.*
die	I was sad when my pet turtle got sick and I thought he would . . . *die.*
dying	My beautiful flowers got too much water and are . . . *dying.*

- Have students go back and read the whole words in the column.

❸ MULTISYLLABIC WORDS

For each word, have students read the syllables, then the whole word. Use the word in a sentence, as appropriate.

complicated	The problem was hard to figure out. It was . . . *complicated.*
popsicle	It was so hot, I wanted an ice-cold banana . . . *popsicle.*
gremlin	A make-believe creature that causes problems is a . . . *gremlin.*
funeral	When our dog died, we buried him and held a . . . *funeral.*
kindling	We started the fire with small sticks and dry leaves. We started the fire with . . . *kindling.*
compost	Some people put their food scraps into a . . . *compost . . .* bucket.

❹ NAMES

❺ GENERALIZATION: READING NEW WORDS IN PARAGRAPHS

- Have students read the paragraph silently, then out loud. Tell students to use the sounds and word parts they know to read any difficult words.
- Repeat practice, as needed.

Judy Moody Saves the World!

Unit 24 Exercise 3
Use before Chapter 3

1. SOUND PRACTICE In each column, have students spell and say the sound, next say any underlined sound and the word, then read the column.

ue, ew, u_e	-dge, ge, gi	-y as in baby	Mixed Practice
gl<u>ue</u>	tru<u>dg</u>ed	mush<u>y</u>	t<u>oi</u>let
ch<u>ew</u>ing	plun<u>g</u>er	leak<u>y</u>	r<u>ui</u>n
re<u>u</u>se	garbolo<u>gi</u>st	energ<u>y</u>	b<u>i</u>ke

2. ACCURACY/FLUENCY BUILDING For each column, have students say any underlined part, then read each word. Next, have them read the column.

A1 Contractions	B1 Compound Words	C1 Multisyllabic Words	D1 Word Endings	E1 Tricky Words
it will	lipstick	chocolate	<u>hater</u>	oxygen
it'll	makeup	vanilla	<u>clomped</u>	warming
	eggshells	muffin	<u>spying</u>	sorry
has not	flashlight	coffee	<u>grinding</u>	
hasn't	cupboard	brownie	<u>smooshed</u>	die
	tiptoed	honey	<u>spices</u>	dying
what is		Kindergarten		
what's				

BUILDING INDEPENDENCE (Reminder)

Some students will try to follow your voice instead of learning to read the sounds and words. Therefore, it is important for you to demonstrate and guide practice only as needed.

Give students many opportunities to respond without your assistance—with groups and individuals. Encourage independence.

3. MULTISYLLABIC WORDS Have students read each word part, then read each whole word.

Ⓐ	com•pli•cat•ed	complicated	pop•si•cle	popsicle
Ⓑ	grem•lin	gremlin	fu•ner•al	funeral
Ⓒ	kin•dling	kindling	com•post	compost

4. NAMES Have students use the sounds and word parts they know to figure out the words.

Laura Ingalls Wilder	Scarlett O'Cherry	Sleeping Beauty	Mr. Rubbish

5. GENERALIZATION Have students read the paragraph silently, then out loud. (New words: pollution, affects, global, gooey, lollipop)

Mrs. Todd was driving the class on a field trip to the new museum. All the kids were excited and talking. The kids were going to learn about how pollution affects the global weather. Before entering the museum, Mrs. Todd said, "Judy, get rid of that gooey lollipop. No eating in the museum."

40

COMPREHENSION PROCESSES

Understand, Apply

PROCEDURES

Introducing Vocabulary

recycle ★ ruin ★ global warming, oxygen ★ complicated

- For each vocabulary word, have students read the word by parts, then read the whole word.
- Read the student-friendly explanations to students as they follow with their fingers. Then have students use the vocabulary word by following the gray text.
- Review and discuss the illustrations.

  Note: Student vocabulary pages for this unit are found in the students' *Exercise Book 4*.

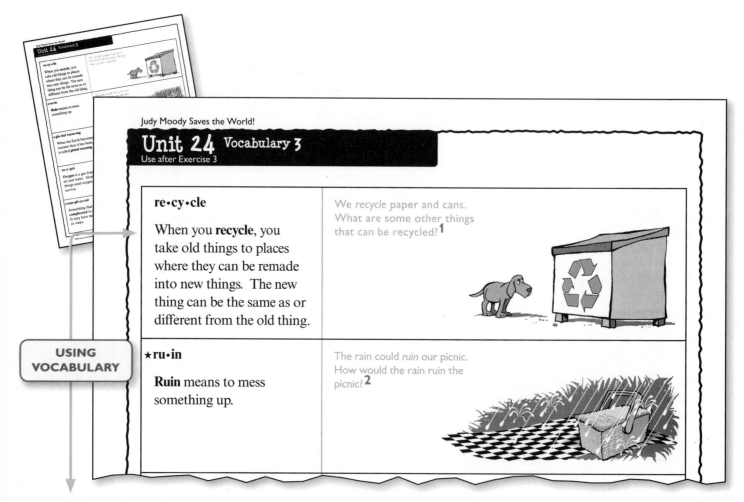

USING VOCABULARY

Judy Moody Saves the World!

Unit 24 Vocabulary 3
Use after Exercise 3

re·cy·cle

When you **recycle**, you take old things to places where they can be remade into new things. The new thing can be the same as or different from the old thing.

We *recycle* paper and cans. What are some other things that can be recycled?[1]

★ru·in

Ruin means to mess something up.

The rain could *ruin* our picnic. How would the rain ruin the picnic?[2]

❶ **Apply:** Using Vocabulary—recycle (We can recycle bottles, plastic bags, and cardboard.)

❷ **Apply:** Using Vocabulary—ruin (The rain would ruin the picnic by getting the food all wet.)

★ = New in this unit

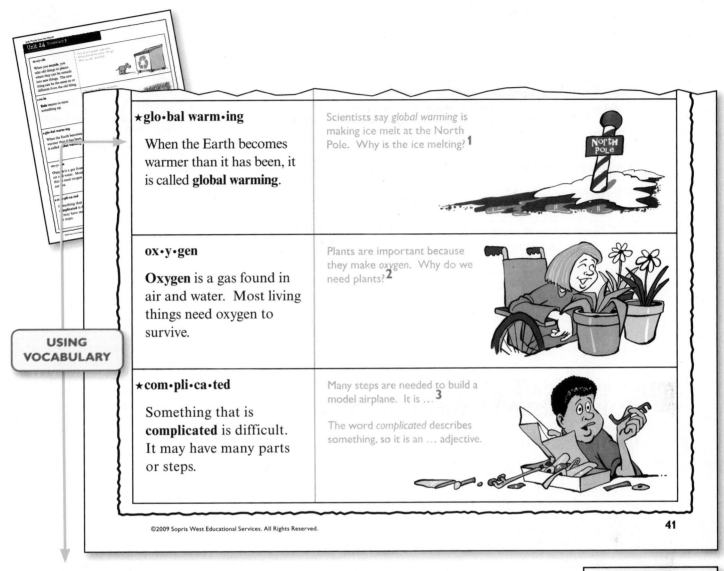

USING VOCABULARY

★glo·bal warm·ing

When the Earth becomes warmer than it has been, it is called **global warming**.

Scientists say *global warming* is making ice melt at the North Pole. Why is the ice melting?**1**

ox·y·gen

Oxygen is a gas found in air and water. Most living things need oxygen to survive.

Plants are important because they make *oxygen*. Why do we need plants?**2**

★com·pli·ca·ted

Something that is **complicated** is difficult. It may have many parts or steps.

Many steps are needed to build a model airplane. It is …**3**

The word *complicated* describes something, so it is an … adjective.

41

❶ **Apply:** Using Vocabulary—global warming (The ice is melting because of global warming.)
❷ **Understand:** Using Vocabulary—oxygen (We need plants because they make oxygen. We need oxygen to breathe.)
❸ **Understand:** Using Vocabulary—complicated (complicated)

USING VOCABULARY

Be enthusiastic about learning new words. Keep a running list of words you would like to use and encourage students to use. Keep the list handy when you are teaching. Put students' names on the board to acknowledge use of a word. Say things like:
Wow! [Alicia] used the word *recycle* when she was talking about the newspaper drive. What a great way to use a vocabulary word!

STORY READING INSTRUCTIONS

Students read Chapter 3 (A Mr. Rubbish Mood) pages 26–33 with the teacher and pages 34–41 on their own.

COMPREHENSION PROCESSES

Remember, Understand, Apply, Analyze, Evaluate

PROCEDURES

1. Reviewing Chapter 2 (Batty for Banana Peels)

Summarizing—Problem, What, Goal; Using Vocabulary—recycle, compost, energy

Discuss students' questions and any other interesting things they found out about Judy. Also discuss the questions from Chapter 2, Setting a Purpose. Say something like:

At the beginning of Chapter 2, what was Judy's problem?
(She couldn't think of an idea for the contest.)

What was Judy's idea for the Crazy Strip Contest? (Her idea was "Heal the World.")
Why did Judy want Rocky to eat bananas?
(So they would have banana peels to put in their compost bucket.)
What did Judy mean when she said, "There's going to be a few changes around here"?
(She wants the family to help save the Earth. She wants them to recycle, compost, and save energy.)

> **CORRECTING DECODING ERRORS**
> During story reading, gently correct any error, then have students reread the sentence.

2. Introducing Chapter 3 (A Mr. Rubbish Mood)

Identifying—Title; Inferring; Defining Vocabulary—mood

Have students read the chapter title. Say something like:

What's the title of this chapter? (A Mr. Rubbish Mood)
What could that mean? A mood is . . . how you feel.
Rubbish is another word for *garbage*.
How do you think you would feel if you were in a Mr. Rubbish mood?
(I would feel bad, like rubbish, like garbage . . .)
Let's read to find out who Mr. Rubbish is!

3. First Reading

- Ask questions and discuss the story as indicated by the blue text in this guide.
- Mix group and individual turns, independent of your voice.
  Have students work toward a group accuracy goal of 0–6 errors.
  Quietly keep track of errors made by all students in the group.
- After reading the story, practice any difficult words.
  Reread the story if students have not reached the accuracy goal.

> **REPEATED READINGS**
> **Prosody**
> On the second reading, students practice developing prosody—phrasing and expression. Research has shown that prosody is related to both fluency and comprehension.

4. Second Reading, Short Passage Practice: Developing Prosody

- Demonstrate expressive, fluent reading of the first paragraph on page 26.
- Guide practice with your voice.
- Provide individual turns while others track with their fingers and whisper read.
- Repeat with one paragraph or page at a time, as time allows.

A Mr. Rubbish Mood

It was still dark out when Judy woke up early the next morning. She found her flashlight and notebook. Then she tiptoed downstairs to the kitchen and started to save the world.

She hoped she could save the world before breakfast. Judy wondered if other people making the world a better place had to do it quietly, and in the dark, so their parents would not wake up.

26

After Reading Pages 26 and 27

❶ **Understand:** Explaining
Why did Judy get up early?
(She was going to save the world.)

❷ **Evaluate:** Making Judgments; **Apply:**
Using Vocabulary—impossible
Judy hoped to save the world before breakfast. Do you think she'll be able to do that? Why or why not?
(No, there's not enough time before breakfast. It's impossible.)

After Reading Page 28

❶ Remember: Identifying—Who
Who is Mr. Rubbish?
(Mr. Rubbish is the Good Garbage Gremlin, a character in Stink's comic book.)

❷ Understand: Explaining—Character Traits (Characterization); Using Vocabulary—recycle
What was Mr. Rubbish like?
(Mr. Rubbish recycled everything. He didn't use anything from the rain forest.)

❸ Analyze: Drawing Conclusions, Inferring
Why was the chapter called
"A Mr. Rubbish Mood"?
(Judy felt like Mr. Rubbish because she wanted to save the environment too.)
Is a Mr. Rubbish mood a good mood or a bad mood?
(It's a good mood.)
Right, it's a good thing. It isn't what we thought it would be.

After Reading Page 29

❶ Remember: Identifying—What
What things come from the rain forest?
(rubber, chocolate, spices, gum, coffee beans . . .)

❷ Analyze: Drawing Conclusions; **Apply:** Using Vocabulary—environment
Why did Judy think her family shouldn't use things that come from the rain forest?
(You have to cut down many trees to grow coffee and make things. Cutting down trees is not good for the environment.)

❸ Apply: Inferring
How do you think Judy's family will feel about not using things from the rain forest?
(They probably won't be very happy about giving up some of their favorite things . . .)

PG 30   PG 31

After Viewing Pages 30 and 31

❶ **Understand:** Identifying—What
Name three of the rain forest products on the table.
(chocolate, rubber bands, gumballs . . .)

❷ **Apply:** Inferring; Using Vocabulary—
distressed, confused
How do you think Stink and his mom feel about
what Judy is doing?
(Stink looks distressed, and his mom
looks confused.)

After Reading Pages 32 and 33

❶ **Analyze:** Drawing Conclusions
What did Judy's family think about her idea? How can you tell?
(They didn't like it. They took their things back.)

❷ **Understand:** Explaining
What was Judy's Plan B?
(She would show her family how much they hurt the planet by writing down everything they threw away.)

❸ **Apply:** Inferring; Explaining
How will that help save the Earth?
(It will show how much they throw away, so maybe they will want to stop wasting so much.)

❹ **Analyze:** Drawing Conclusions
Do you think Plan B will work? Why or why not?
(Yes, I think Plan B will work because they will be embarrassed when they see how much they throw away. Then they will stop wasting so much. No, Judy will just waste time and paper and make her family mad.)

CHAPTER 3 INSTRUCTIONS

Students read pages 34–41 without the teacher, independently or with partners.

COMPREHENSION PROCESSES

Remember, Analyze, Evaluate

PROCEDURES FOR READING ON YOUR OWN

1. Getting Ready

Have students turn to page 34.

2. Setting a Purpose

Summarizing—Goals, Facts; Note Taking

Before students begin reading, say something like:

Let's review Judy's goals. What was her first goal?

(Her first goal was to win the Crazy Strips contest.)

Now she has another goal. What is it?

(She wants to save the world.)

That's right. I think we are going to learn more about how she plans to save the world. As you read, think about these things:

- How much garbage does one person throw away every day?
- Name three reasons trees are important to the Earth.
- List some of the things Judy did to help save the world.

> **PREP NOTE**
>
> **Setting a Purpose**
>
> Write questions on a chalkboard, white board, or large piece of paper before working with your small group.

PG **41**

3. Reading on Your Own: Partner or Whisper Reading

- Have students take turns reading every other page with a partner or have students whisper read pages 34–41 on their own.
- Continue having students track each word with their fingers.

4. Comprehension and Skill Work

Tell students that after they read on their own, they will do Comprehension and Skill Activity 3, write their third letter to Judy, and draw her mood on the cover. Guide practice, as needed. For teacher directions, see pages 50 and 51.

5. Homework 3: New Passage

VOCABULARY LOG

COMPREHENSION PROCESSES

Understand, Apply

WRITING TRAITS

Conventions—Complete Sentence, Capital, Period
Presentation

> **Defining and Using Vocabulary—**
> **outrageous, moody, mood, creative**
> **Illustrating; Sentence Completion**

Judy Moody Saves the World!

Unit 24 Activity 3

Name _____

Vocabulary Log

(Accept any reasonable response.)

Word	Definition	Sentence	Picture
outrageous	Something that is outrageous is very shocking, different.	She had an outrageous hat!	
moody	Someone who is moody has many different moods.	You seem kind of moody today.	
mood	A mood is _a feeling._ It can be happy, sad, mad, or silly.	At the end of Chapter 3, Judy thinks her family doesn't understand her. This put Judy in a bad mood.	
creative	Someone who is creative is very good at using their imagination.	The drawing you drew is very creative.	

©2009 Sopris West Educational Services. All Rights Reserved.

61

PROCEDURES

For each step, demonstrate and guide practice, as needed. Then have students complete the page independently.

Vocabulary: Sentence Writing—Specific Instructions

- Have students read the vocabulary words and complete the definitions.
- Have students write a sentence using each vocabulary word. Remind them to start with a capital and end with a period.
- Have students draw a picture in the box to illustrate their sentence.

ENTRIES 3a, 3b

COMPREHENSION PROCESSES

Understand, Evaluate, Create

WRITING TRAITS

Ideas and Content
Word Choice
Conventions—Complete Sentence,
Capital, Period
Presentation

Generating Ideas, Responding
Making Lists, Sentence Completion

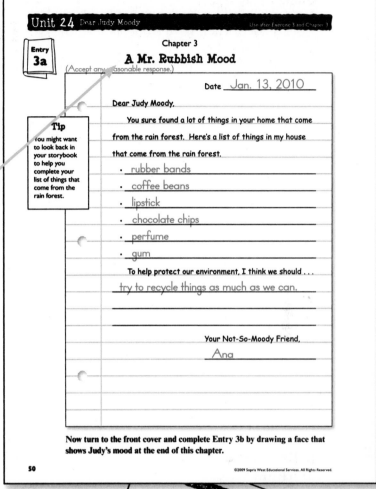

PROCEDURES

Have students complete the page independently. Guide practice, only as needed.

Letter Writing: Creative Writing—Specific Instructions (Entry 3a)

Have students fill in the blanks to complete a letter to Judy Moody. Encourage them to look back in their storybook, if needed, to complete their list. Remind them to start sentences with a capital and end with a period.

Cover: Illustrating—Specific Instructions (Entry 3b)

Have students find the box labeled Entry 3b and draw a face that shows Judy's mood at the end of this chapter. Remind them to look back in their book, if needed.

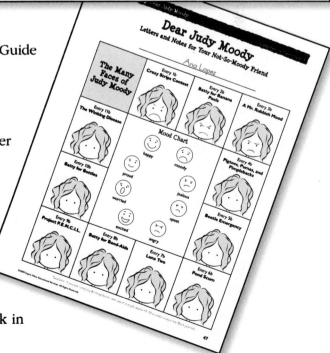

① SOUND REVIEW
Use selected Sound Cards from Units 1–19.

② ACCURACY AND FLUENCY BUILDING
- For each task, have students say any underlined part, then read the word.
- Set a pace. Then have students read the whole words in each task and column.
- Provide repeated practice, building accuracy first, then fluency.

E1. Tricky Words
- For each Tricky Word, have students use the sounds and word parts they know to silently sound out the word. Use the word in a sentence to help with pronunciation.

species	Did you know the panda bear is an endangered . . . *species?*
straight	Jillian's hair is curly, but she wishes it were . . . *straight.*
honor	The Lincoln Memorial was built in . . . *honor* . . . of Abraham Lincoln.
toes	Most people have ten fingers and ten . . . *toes.*
tour	When my family went to Los Angeles, we took a city . . . *tour.*

- Have students go back and read the whole words in the column.

③ MULTISYLLABIC WORDS
For each word, have students read the syllables, then the whole word. Use the word in a sentence, as appropriate.

specimen	The slug was a particularly slimy . . . *specimen.*
extremely	The kids went swimming on Saturday because it was . . . *extremely* . . . hot.
collection	Jaden likes comics about superheroes. He has an entire . . . *collection.*
sluggy	A made-up word that means yucky and like a slug is . . . *sluggy.*
polish	If you want your shoes to shine, you need to . . . *polish* . . . them.
arachnid	A spider is an . . . *arachnid.*
pajama	Bette has pictures of a sleepy bear on her . . . *pajama* . . . top.
introduced	I didn't come onto the stage until after I was . . . *introduced.*

④ WORDS IN CONTEXT
For each word, have students use the sounds and word parts they know to silently sound out the word. Then have students read the sentence. Assist, as needed.

★⑤ ENDANGERED SPECIES
- Tell students these are the names of endangered species they will read about in the story.
- Have students use the sounds and word parts they know to figure out the words. Assist, as needed.

⑥ GENERALIZATION: READING NEW WORDS IN PARAGRAPHS
- Have students read the paragraph silently, then out loud. Tell students to use the sounds and word parts they know to read any difficult words.
- Repeat practice, as needed.

MULTISYLLABIC WORDS CORRECTION PROCEDURE
If students make an error, put the word on the board. Draw loops under each syllable and guide practice with your hand. Have students say each syllable then read the whole word.

★ = New in this unit

Judy Moody Saves the World!

Unit 24 Exercise 4
Use before Chapter 4

1. SOUND REVIEW Use selected Sound Cards from Units 1–19.

2. ACCURACY/FLUENCY BUILDING For each column, have students say any underlined part, then read each word. Next, have them read the column.

A1 Mixed Practice	B1 Compound Words	C1 Names and Places	D1 Word Endings	E1 Tricky Words
l<u>ice</u>	smartypants	Smithsonian	<u>squirm</u>ed	species
l<u>ou</u>se	pigtoe	Bullwinkle	<u>shack</u>ing	straight
s<u>ow</u> bug	pillbuggy	Washington, D.C.	<u>adopt</u>ed	honor
glued		Ms. Stickley	<u>depend</u>s	toes
ch<u>oi</u>ces			<u>magazine</u>s	tour

3. MULTISYLLABIC WORDS Have students read each word part, then read each whole word. For Row C, have students read each whole word.

A	spe•ci•men	specimen	ex•treme•ly	extremely
B	col•lec•tion	collection	slug•gy	sluggy
C	polish	arachnid	pajama	introduced

4. WORDS IN CONTEXT Have students use the sounds they know and then the sentences to pronounce each underlined word.

A	crus•ta•ceans (krus-tay-shuns)	Lobster, shrimp, crabs, and lice are <u>crustaceans</u>.
B	i•so•pod (ice-o-pod) 	An <u>isopod</u> is a small crustacean with seven pairs of legs.

★5. ENDANGERED SPECIES Have students use the sounds and word parts they know to figure out the words.

A	leatherback sea turtle	northeast beach tiger beetle	nocturnal aye-ayes
B	pimpleback pearlymussel	Virginia fringed mountain snail	shortnose sturgeon

6. GENERALIZATION Have students read the paragraph silently, then out loud. (New words: Stephanie, Randi, dismal, shrew, pumas)

Stephanie and her friend, Randi, are studying endangered species in their science class. Stephanie is writing a paper on the Dismal Swamp shrew. The shrew is a cute little mammal with a long snout. Randi is writing about pumas, a large cat of the American continents.

COMPREHENSION PROCESSES

Understand, Apply

PROCEDURES

Introducing Vocabulary

> ☆ **crack someone up, endangered** ☆ **endangered species** ☆ **adopt, environment**

- For each vocabulary word, have students read the word by parts, then read the whole word.
- Read the student-friendly explanations to students as they follow with their fingers. Then have students use the vocabulary word by following the gray text.
- Review and discuss the illustrations.
  Note: Student vocabulary pages for this unit are found in the students' *Exercise Book 4*.

USING VOCABULARY

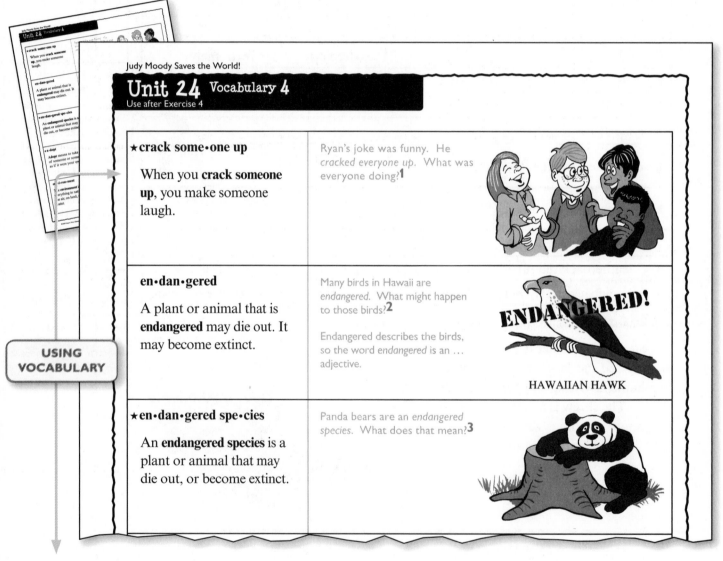

Judy Moody Saves the World!

Unit 24 Vocabulary 4
Use after Exercise 4

★ **crack some·one up**

When you **crack someone up**, you make someone laugh.

Ryan's joke was funny. He *cracked everyone up.* What was everyone doing?**1**

en·dan·gered

A plant or animal that is **endangered** may die out. It may become extinct.

Many birds in Hawaii are *endangered.* What might happen to those birds?**2**

Endangered describes the birds, so the word *endangered* is an … adjective.

ENDANGERED!

HAWAIIAN HAWK

★ **en·dan·gered spe·cies**

An **endangered species** is a plant or animal that may die out, or become extinct.

Panda bears are an *endangered species.* What does that mean?**3**

❶ **Apply:** Making Connections; Using Vocabulary—crack someone up (Everyone was laughing really hard.)

❷ **Apply:** Using Vocabulary—endangered (Those birds might die out.)

❸ **Apply:** Using Vocabulary—endangered species (Panda bears may become extinct.)

☆ = New in this unit

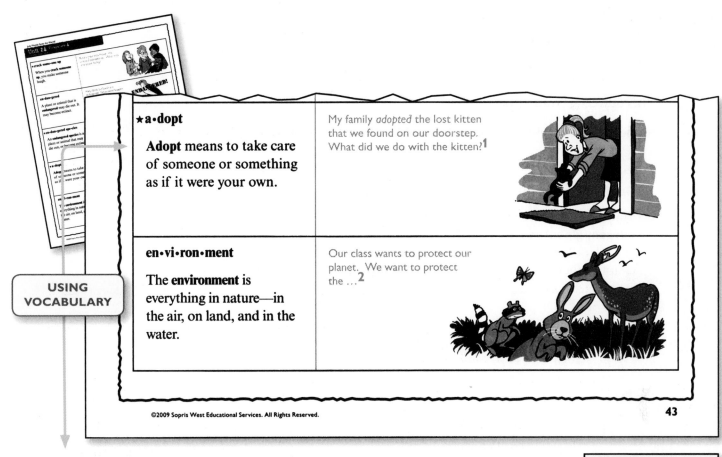

USING VOCABULARY

43

❶ **Apply:** Making Connections; Using Vocabulary—adopt (We took care of the kitten.)

❷ **Understand:** Using Vocabulary—environment, protect (environment)

> **USING VOCABULARY**
>
> Be enthusiastic about learning new words. Keep a running list of words you would like to use and encourage students to use. Keep the list handy when you are teaching. Put students' names on the board to acknowledge use of a word. Say things like:
>
> [Shannon] used *endangered species* when she was talking about pandas. What a brilliant way to use a vocabulary word!

STORY READING INSTRUCTIONS

Students read Chapter 4 (Pigtoes, Pumas, and Pimplebacks), pages 42–48 (top of page) with the teacher and 48–54 on their own. Page 48 is split between reading sessions.

COMPREHENSION PROCESSES

Remember, Understand, Apply, Evaluate

PROCEDURES

1. Reviewing Chapter 3 (A Mr. Rubbish Mood)

Summarizing; Locating Information; Identifying—Facts; Inferring; Using Vocabulary— oxygen, global warming, discouraged, determined, planet

Have students turn to page 26. Quickly review what happened in the first part of the chapter, then discuss the questions from Chapter 3, Setting a Purpose. Say something like: How much garbage does one person throw away every day? Look back to page 35 in your book, if you need to.

(One person throws away eight pounds of garbage.)

Name three reasons trees are important to the Earth.

(Trees give shade. They make oxygen. They help remove dust from the air. They help control global warming . . .)

List some of the things Judy did to help save the world.

(She tried to get rid of things that came from the rain forest. She started writing down everything her family threw away. She saved water by not brushing her teeth . . .)

Why do you think Judy was discouraged at the end of Chapter 3?

(She was discouraged because her family didn't want to help. She was still determined to do what she could to save the planet.)

2. Introducing Chapter 4 (Pigtoes, Pumas, and Pimplebacks)

Identifying—Title; Predicting

Discuss the title. Say something like:

Turn to page 42. What's the title of the chapter? (Pigtoes, Pumas, and Pimplebacks)

That's a funny title. I'll give you a hint. Those are different kinds of animals.

What do you think we'll be reading about in this chapter? (We'll read about animals.)

3. First Reading

- Ask questions and discuss the story as indicated by the blue text in this guide.
- Mix group and individual turns, independent of your voice.
  Have students work toward a group accuracy goal of 0–6 errors.
- After reading the story, practice any difficult words.
  Reread the story if students have not reached the accuracy goal.

4. Second Reading, Timed Readings: Repeated Reading

- As time allows, have students do Timed Readings while others follow along.
- Time individuals for 30 seconds and encourage each child to work for a personal best.
- Determine words correct per minute. Record student scores.

Pigtoes, Pumas, and Pimplebacks

At school, Judy wiggled all during Math in the morning. She squirmed through Spelling. At last it was Science.

"Over half the world's plants and animals are found in rain forests," Mr. Todd said. "Which is why it's so important to protect the rain forest. The health of our whole planet depends on it. But did you know that there are endangered species right here in Virginia?"

42

After Reading Page 42

❶ **Apply:** Inferring, Explaining
Why was Judy eager to get to science class?
(She wanted to learn more about saving the world.)

❷ **Apply:** Making Connections; Using Vocabulary— endangered, extinct
An endangered species is an animal or plant in danger of becoming extinct. Can you think of an animal we've read about that is extinct?
(Dinosaurs are extinct.)

PG 45

After Reading Page 43

❶ **Understand:** Explaining; Using Vocabulary—endangered species
Each student in Judy's class will adopt an endangered species in their state. What will they do for their animal?
(They will tell the class about their animal, why it's endangered, and how to help it.)

After Reading Page 44

❶ **Remember:** Identifying—What
What were some of the endangered species that were adopted by kids in Judy's class?
(They adopted the bald eagle, the Shenandoah salamander, the puma, the monkeyface mussel, the leatherback sea turtle . . .)

❷ **Evaluate:** Responding
If you were in Judy's class, which animal would you want to do your report on?
(The monkeyface mussel sounds like fun . . .)

After Viewing Page 45

❶ **Apply:** Viewing; Inferring; Explaining; Using Vocabulary—mood, frustrated
Look at the picture of Judy. What kind of mood do you think she is in?
(She looks frustrated because Mr. Todd isn't calling on her . . .)

After Reading Page 46

❶ **Remember:** Identifying—What;
Using Vocabulary—adopt
What animal did Judy adopt?
(She adopted the northeast beach tiger beetle.)

❷ **Apply:** Inferring
How did Judy feel about her animal?
(She didn't like it.)

❸ **Apply:** Inferring; Explaining; Using Vocabulary—trade
How can you tell she didn't like her animal?
(She wanted to trade.)

After Reading Pages 47 and 48

❶ **Remember:** Identifying—Where
Where did Mr. Todd tell them to look for more information about their animals?
(He told them to look in the library, on the Internet, and at the museum.)

❷ **Understand:** Identifying—What
What kind of museum will Judy's class visit?
(They'll visit a little science museum.)

STORY READING INSTRUCTIONS

Students read pages 48–54 without the teacher, independently or with partners.

COMPREHENSION PROCESSES

Remember, Understand, Apply

PROCEDURES FOR READING ON YOUR OWN

1. **Getting Ready**

   Have students turn to page 48 and find the first line after the divider.

2. **Setting a Purpose**

   Identifying—Who, What; Inferring

   Before students begin reading, say something like:

   On your own, read to find out what happens when Judy's class goes to the science museum.

   You'll be reading about endangered animals. Stop at the end of the chapter. Some questions for you to think about as you read are on the board.

   - Who was Ms. Stick Bug?
   - What were some of the animals the kids learned about at the museum?
   - Why was Judy worried about her science grade?

3. **Reading on Your Own: Partner or Whisper Reading**

   - Have students take turns reading every other page with a partner or have students whisper read pages 48–54 on their own.
   - Continue having students track each word with their fingers.

4. **Comprehension and Skill Work**

   Tell students that after they read on their own, they will do Comprehension and Skill Activity 4, write to Judy, and do the **Many Faces of Judy Moody** for this chapter. Guide practice, as needed. (For teacher directions, see pages 62 and 63.)

5. **Homework 4: New Passage**

> **PREP NOTE**
>
> **Setting a Purpose**
> Write questions on a chalkboard, white board, or large piece of paper before working with your small group.

STORY COMPREHENSION

COMPREHENSION PROCESSES
Remember, Understand, Analyze

WRITING TRAITS
Conventions—Complete Sentence, Capital, Period
Presentation

Identifying—What

Identifying—Where

Identifying—Action

Inferring; Defining and Using Vocabulary—endangered

Using Graphic Organizer
Using Vocabulary—mood, unsettled

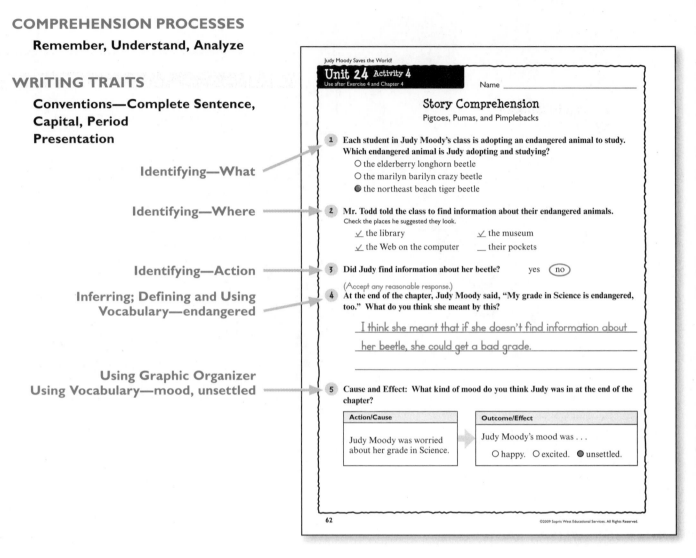

Judy Moody Saves the World!

Unit 24 Activity 4
Use after Exercise 4 and Chapter 4

Name _____

Story Comprehension
Pigtoes, Pumas, and Pimplebacks

1. Each student in Judy Moody's class is adopting an endangered animal to study. Which endangered animal is Judy adopting and studying?
   - ○ the elderberry longhorn beetle
   - ○ the marilyn barilyn crazy beetle
   - ● the northeast beach tiger beetle

2. Mr. Todd told the class to find information about their endangered animals. Check the places he suggested they look.
   - ✓ the library   ✓ the museum
   - ✓ the Web on the computer   __ their pockets

3. Did Judy find information about her beetle?   yes   (no)

   (Accept any reasonable response.)

4. At the end of the chapter, Judy Moody said, "My grade in Science is endangered, too." What do you think she meant by this?

   I think she meant that if she doesn't find information about her beetle, she could get a bad grade.

5. Cause and Effect: What kind of mood do you think Judy was in at the end of the chapter?

Action/Cause	Outcome/Effect
Judy Moody was worried about her grade in Science.	Judy Moody's mood was . . . ○ happy. ○ excited. ● unsettled.

62   ©2009 Sopris West Educational Services. All Rights Reserved.

PROCEDURES

For each step, demonstrate and guide practice, as needed. Then have students complete the page independently.

1. **Selection Response—Basic Instructions** (Items 1–3)
   Have students read the sentence starters, then fill in the bubble with the correct answer, check all correct answers, or circle the correct answer.

2. **Answering Questions: Sentence Writing—Specific Instructions** (Item 4)
   Have students read the question and write their answer in the blank. Remind students to start their sentences with a capital and end with a period.

3. **Cause/Effect: Sequence Chart—Specific Instructions** (Item 5)
   Have students read the action and complete the outcome by filling in the bubble with the correct answer.

Self-monitoring
Have students check and correct their work.

ENTRIES 4a, 4b

COMPREHENSION PROCESSES

Understand, Create

WRITING TRAITS

Ideas and Content
Word Choice
Conventions—Complete Sentence,
Capital, Period
Presentation

> Generating Ideas, Asking Questions
> Making Lists, Sentence Completion

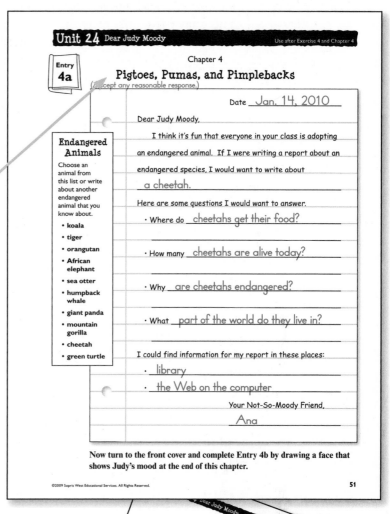

SPECIAL NOTE

Your students will complete a Dear Judy Moody book. For ease of use, pull pages 47–58 from *Activity Book 4*. Staple the pages together into a book.

PROCEDURES

Have students complete the page independently. Guide practice, only as needed.

Letter Writing: Creative Writing—Specific Instructions (Entry 4a)

- Have students read the names of the endangered animals in the box.
- Have students pick an endangered animal, then fill in the blanks to complete a letter to Judy Moody.
- Remind them to end sentences with a period and end questions with a question mark.

Cover: Illustrating—Specific Instructions (Entry 4b)

Have students find the box labeled Entry 4b and draw a face that shows Judy's mood at the end of this chapter. Remind them to look back in their book, if needed.

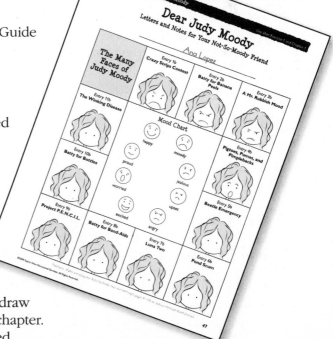

❶ SOUND REVIEW

❷ ACCURACY AND FLUENCY BUILDING
- For each task, have students say any underlined part, then read the word.
- Set a pace. Then have students read the whole words in each task and column.
- Provide repeated practice, building accuracy first, then fluency.

C1. Multisyllabic Words
- For the list of words divided by syllables, have students read each syllable, then the whole word. Use the word in a sentence, as appropriate.
- For the list of whole words, build accuracy and then fluency.

mascot	The football team has a bulldog for a . . . *mascot.*
shoreline	We found lots of seashells along the . . . *shoreline.*
stubborn	Mules are known to be very . . . *stubborn.*
ozone	The Earth is protected from the sun's harmful rays by . . . *ozone.*
emergency	The police turned on their sirens as they drove to the . . . *emergency.*
development	The reporter was interested in the latest . . . *development.*
endangered	Many animals have lost their habitat and are . . . *endangered.*

D1. Tricky Words
- For each Tricky Word, have students use the sounds and word parts they know to silently sound out the word. Use the word in a sentence to help with pronunciation.

encyclopedia	I wanted to know about Asia, so I looked it up in an . . . *encyclopedia.*
shrieked	When Hannah saw the spider on her shirt, she . . . *shrieked.*
species	There are thousands of different animal and plant . . . *species.*
areas	There are tidepools in many coastal . . . *areas.*
double	The two boys looked identical. I thought I must be seeing . . . *double.*
searched	The thief's pockets were . . . *searched.*
recycled	The kids took the cans to the store to be . . . *recycled.*

- Have students go back and read the whole words in the column.

❸ WORDS IN CONTEXT
For each word, have students use the sounds and word parts they know to silently sound out the word. Then have students read the sentence. Assist, as needed.

❹ MORPHOGRAPHS AND AFFIXES

❺ ENDANGERED SPECIES
- Tell students these are the names of endangered species they will read about in the story.
- Have students use the sounds and word parts they know to figure out the words. Assist, as needed.

❻ GENERALIZATION: READING NEW WORDS IN PARAGRAPHS
Have students read the paragraph silently, then out loud. Tell students to use the sounds and word parts they know to read any difficult words.

Note: Encyclopedia is spelled "encyclopaedia" in Unit 19. Both spellings are acceptable.

Judy Moody Saves the World!

Unit 24 Exercise 5
Use before Chapters 5

1. SOUND REVIEW Use selected Sound Cards from Units 1–19.

2. ACCURACY/FLUENCY BUILDING For each column, have students say any underlined part, then read each word. Next, have them read the column.

A1 Names and Places	**B1** Word Endings	**C1** Multisyllabic Words		**D1** Tricky Words
Cinderella	<u>wrapper</u>	mas·cot	mascot	encyclopedia
Hercules	<u>capitals</u>	shore·line	shoreline	shrieked
Chesapeake	<u>pajamas</u>	stub·born	stubborn	species
Latin	<u>beaches</u>	o·zone	ozone	areas
	<u>adopts</u>	e·mer·gen·cy	emergency	double
		de·vel·op·ment	development	searched
	paste	en·dan·gered	endangered	recycled
	pasting			

3. WORDS IN CONTEXT Have students use the sounds they know and then the sentences to pronounce each underlined word.

Ⓐ e·ro·sion <u>Erosion</u> caused the hillside to gradually slide down the slope.

Ⓑ ga·zil·lion I couldn't count the mosquitoes. There were a <u>gazillion</u> of them.

4. MORPHOGRAPHS AND AFFIXES Have students read each underlined part, then the word.

popula<u>tion</u>   collect<u>or</u>   activ<u>ity</u>   dic<u>tion</u>ary

5. ENDANGERED SPECIES Have students use the sounds and word parts they know and the pronunciation guide to figure out the words.

Ⓐ Cicindela dorsalis dorsalis   se-sin-de-la dor-sa-lis dor-sa-lis
<u>Cicindela dorsalis dorsalis</u> is the species name of the northeast beach tiger beetle.

Ⓑ   monkeyface mussel   elderberry longhorn beetle   dung beetle

6. GENERALIZATION Have students read the paragraph silently, then out loud. (New words: Beatles, McCartney, Lennon)

A famous rock band during the 1960s was The Beatles. One of the singers was Paul McCartney. John Lennon was another member of the band. They were from England.

GRADUALLY INCREASE STUDENT RESPONSE RATE (Reminder)

After students are accurate, gradually increase the rate of response. Demonstrate and guide a pace slightly faster than the students' rate.

COMPREHENSION PROCESSES

Apply

PROCEDURES

Introducing Vocabulary

habitat ☆ mascot ☆ ignore ☆ ozone ☆ good cause ☆ stubborn

- For each vocabulary word, have students read the word by parts, then read the whole word.
- Read the student-friendly explanations to students as they follow with their fingers. Then have students use the vocabulary word by following the gray text.
- Review and discuss the photo and illustrations.
  Note: Student vocabulary pages for this unit are found in the students' *Exercise Book 4*.

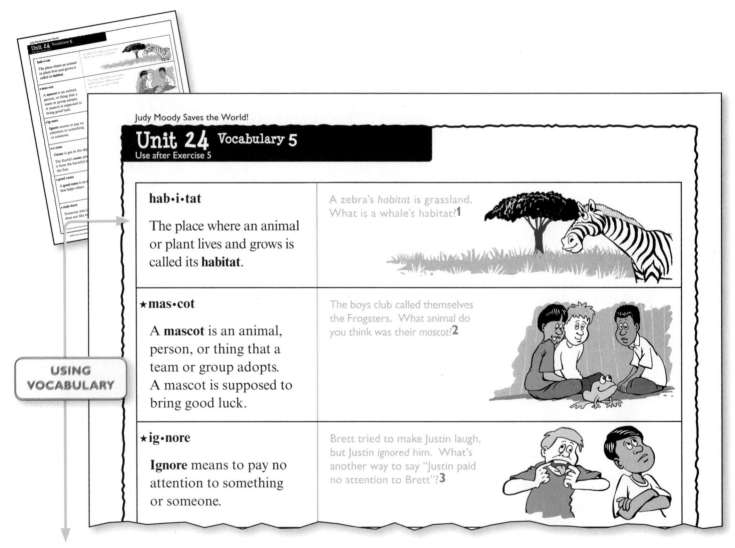

Judy Moody Saves the World!

Unit 24 Vocabulary 5
Use after Exercise 5

USING VOCABULARY

hab·i·tat The place where an animal or plant lives and grows is called its **habitat**.	A zebra's *habitat* is grassland. What is a whale's habitat?**1**
★**mas·cot** A **mascot** is an animal, person, or thing that a team or group adopts. A mascot is supposed to bring good luck.	The boys club called themselves the Frogsters. What animal do you think was their *mascot*?**2**
★**ig·nore** **Ignore** means to pay no attention to something or someone.	Brett tried to make Justin laugh, but Justin *ignored* him. What's another way to say "Justin paid no attention to Brett"?**3**

❶ **Apply:** Using Vocabulary—habitat (A whale's habitat is the ocean.)
❷ **Apply:** Making Connections; Using Vocabulary—mascot (They probably had a frog as their mascot.)
❸ **Apply:** Using Vocabulary—ignore (Justin ignored Brett.)

☆ = New in this unit

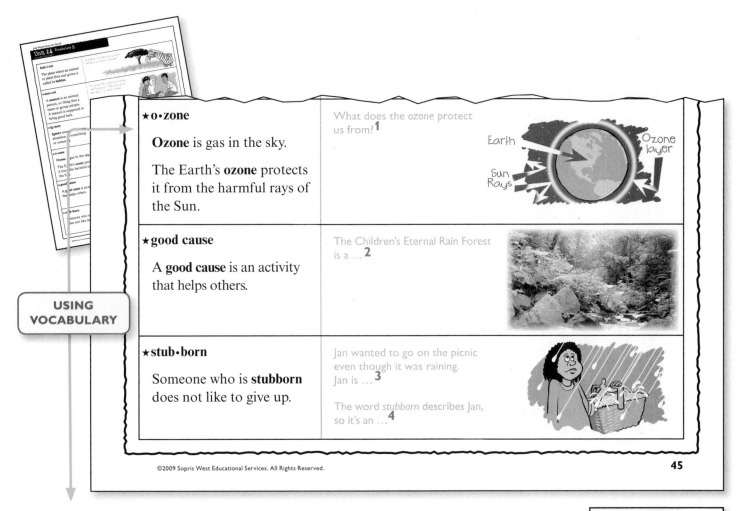

USING VOCABULARY

★**o·zone**

Ozone is gas in the sky.

The Earth's **ozone** protects it from the harmful rays of the Sun.

What does the *ozone* protect us from?[1]

Earth

Ozone layer

Sun Rays

★**good cause**

A **good cause** is an activity that helps others.

The Children's Eternal Rain Forest is a …[2]

★**stub·born**

Someone who is **stubborn** does not like to give up.

Jan wanted to go on the picnic even though it was raining. Jan is …[3]

The word *stubborn* describes Jan, so it's an …[4]

45

❶ **Apply:** Using Vocabulary—ozone, protect (Ozone protects us from the harmful rays of the Sun.)

❷ **Apply:** Using Vocabulary—good cause (good cause)

❸ **Apply:** Making Connections; Using Vocabulary—stubborn (stubborn)

❹ **Analyze:** Classifying (adjective)

USING VOCABULARY

Be enthusiastic about learning new words. Keep a running list of words you would like to use and encourage students to use. Keep the list handy when you are teaching. Put students' names on the board to acknowledge use of a word. Say things like:

[Joanne] used the word *stubborn* when she told us how her little brother didn't want to eat his peas. That's a great way to use a new vocabulary word.

STORY READING INSTRUCTIONS

Students read Chapter 5 (Beetle Emergency) with the teacher.

COMPREHENSION PROCESSES

Remember, Understand, Apply, Analyze, Create

PROCEDURES

1. **Reviewing Chapter 4 (Pigtoes, Pumas, and Pimplebacks)**

   Summarizing; Identifying—Who, What; Inferring

   Have students turn to page 42. Quickly review what happened in the first part of the chapter, then discuss the questions from Chapter 4, Setting a Purpose. Say something like: Yesterday you read part of Chapter 4 your own. Let's see what you found out.
   Who was Ms. Stick Bug?
   (Ms. Stick Bug was the lady at the museum. Her real name was Stephanie Stickley.)
   What were some of the animals the kids learned about at the museum?
   (They learned about the Shenandoah salamander, the Virginia fringed mountain snail . . .)
   Why was Judy worried about her science grade?
   (The museum didn't have a northeast beach tiger beetle. She had no information for her report.)

2. **Introducing Chapter 5 (Beetle Emergency)**

   Identifying—Title; Inferring; Explaining

   Have students read the chapter title.
   What is the title of this chapter? (Beetle Emergency)
   What do you think is the Beetle Emergency?
   (Judy was supposed to do a report on the beetle, but she had no information about it.)

3. **First Reading**
   - Ask questions and discuss the story as indicated by the blue text in this guide.
   - Mixing turns, have students work toward a group accuracy goal of 0–6 errors. Quietly keep track of errors made by all students in the group.
   - After reading the story, practice any difficult words.

4. **Second Reading, Short Passage Practice: Developing Prosody**
   - Demonstrate expressive, fluent reading of the first two paragraphs.
   - Guide practice with your voice.
   - Provide individual turns while others track with their fingers and whisper read.
   - Repeat with one paragraph at a time.

   > **CORRECTING DECODING ERRORS**
   > During story reading, gently correct any error, then have students reread the sentence.

5. **Partner or Whisper Reading: Repeated Reading**

   Before independent work, have students finger track and partner or whisper read.

6. **Comprehension and Skill Work**

   Tell students that they will do Comprehension and Skill Activity 5, write a letter to Judy Moody, and do the Many Faces of Judy Moody for this chapter. Guide practice, as needed. For teacher directions, see pages 72 and 73.

7. **Homework 5: New Passage**

Beetle Emergency

The very next morning, Judy started her own search for a real live northeast beach tiger beetle. Before school, she grabbed a peanut butter jar from the recycling bin and ran out into the backyard. She tapped on tree bark. She crawled through itchy grass. She peered down into the dirt.

"Here, beetle, beetle," called Judy. "Don't be endangered."

55

After Reading Page 55

❶ **Analyze:** Drawing Conclusions; **Apply:** Predicting
Do you think Judy will find a beetle? Why or why not?
(No, the beetle is endangered so there aren't many left. No, the beetle is a beach beetle, but she is looking for it in the grass and dirt.)

PG 56

After Viewing Page 56

❶ **Apply:** Viewing, Inferring; Explaining; Using Vocabulary—mood
Look at the picture. What kind of mood do you think Judy is in?
(She is frustrated because she can't find a beetle. She is worried because she will get a bad grade if she can't find any information about the beetle.)

After Reading Page 57

❶ **Remember:** Identifying—Where
Where did Judy look for information about her beetle?
(She looked in a dictionary, in the encyclopedia, on the computer, and in bug books.)

❷ **Apply:** Inferring
What did she find out about her beetle?
(She didn't find out anything about her beetle.)

After Reading Pages 58 and 59

❶ **Understand:** Explaining
How did Frank help Judy find information about her beetle?
(Frank found a stamp with the beetle on it in his stamp collection. His album had information about the beetle.)

After Reading Pages 60 and 61

❶ Apply: Inferring; Using Vocabulary—habitat
A habitat is the place where something lives and grows. What is the habitat of the northeast beach tiger beetle?
(Its habitat is a sandy beach.)

❷ Understand: Explaining; Using Vocabulary—endangered, habitat
Why was Judy's beetle endangered?
(It was endangered by changes in its habitat, human population, shoreline development, and erosion.)

After Reading Page 62 and 63

❶ Apply: Inferring, Explaining
What did Stink think Judy's beetles looked like?
(He thought they looked like flying footballs.)

❷ Apply: Inferring; Explaining; Using Vocabulary—mood
What do you think Judy's mood was while she worked on her report? Why?
(She was happy that she had information. She thought she did a great job drawing pictures of the beetle . . .)

STORY COMPREHENSION

COMPREHENSION PROCESSES

Remember, Understand, Analyze

WRITING TRAITS

Conventions—Complete Sentence, Capital, Period
Presentation

Explaining; Using Idioms and Expressions—save the day

Identifying—Facts; Test Taking

Using Graphic Organizer
Using Vocabulary—mood
Sentence Completion

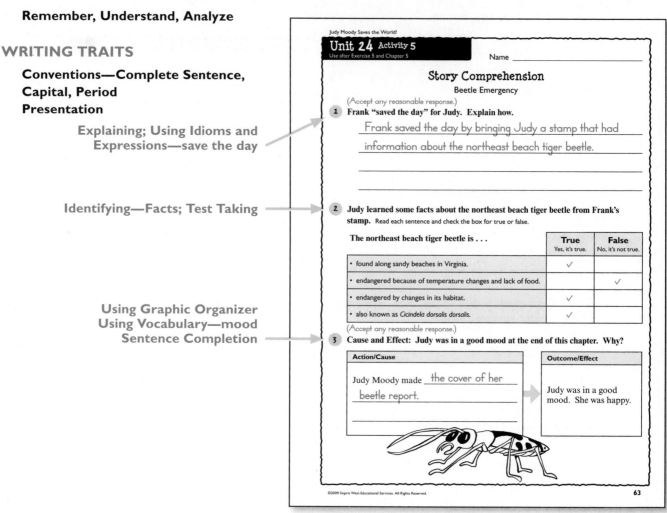

Judy Moody Saves the World!

Unit 24 Activity 5
Use after Exercise 5 and Chapter 5

Name _____

Story Comprehension
Beetle Emergency

(Accept any reasonable response.)

1. Frank "saved the day" for Judy. Explain how.

   Frank saved the day by bringing Judy a stamp that had information about the northeast beach tiger beetle.

2. **Judy learned some facts about the northeast beach tiger beetle from Frank's stamp.** Read each sentence and check the box for true or false.

The northeast beach tiger beetle is . . .	True Yes, it's true.	False No, it's not true.
• found along sandy beaches in Virginia.	✓	
• endangered because of temperature changes and lack of food.		✓
• endangered by changes in its habitat.	✓	
• also known as *Cicindela dorsalis dorsalis*.	✓	

   (Accept any reasonable response.)

3. **Cause and Effect: Judy was in a good mood at the end of this chapter. Why?**

Action/Cause		Outcome/Effect
Judy Moody made the cover of her beetle report.	→	Judy was in a good mood. She was happy.

   ©2009 Sopris West Educational Services. All Rights Reserved.   63

PROCEDURES

For each step, demonstrate and guide practice, as needed. Then have students complete the page independently.

1. **Answering Questions: Sentence Writing—Specific Instructions** (Item 1)
   Have students read the sentences, then write a sentence that explains how Frank "saved the day" for Judy.

2. **True/False: Selection Response** (Item 2)
   Have students read the directions.
   Have students read each item in the list, determine whether the item is true or false, then check the correct box.

3. **Cause/Effect: Sequence Chart—Specific Instructions** (Item 3)
   Have students explain the outcome by completing the sentence in the box in the first column. Remind students to look back in their storybook, if needed.

Self-monitoring
Have students check and correct their work.

ENTRIES 5a, 5b

COMPREHENSION PROCESSES

Understand, Create

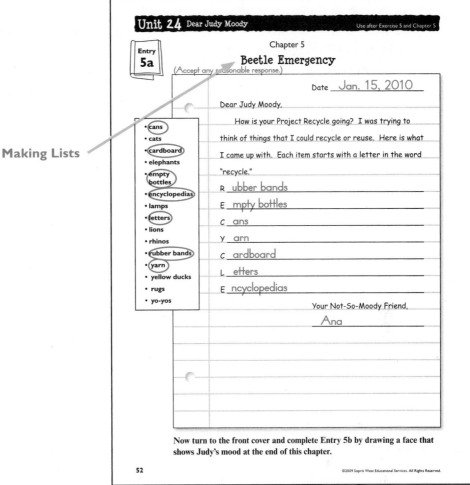

Making Lists

SPECIAL NOTE

Your students will complete a Dear Judy Moody book. For ease of use, pull pages 47–58 from *Activity Book 4*. Staple the pages together into a book.

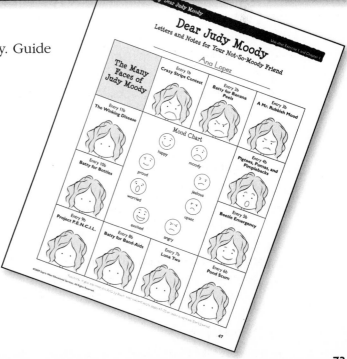

PROCEDURES

Have students complete the page independently. Guide practice, only as needed.

Letter Writing: Making Lists—Specific Instructions (Entry 5a)

Have students read the letter, then select items from the box and write them in the blanks to complete a letter to Judy Moody.

Cover: Illustrating—Specific Instructions (Entry 5b)

Have students find the box labeled Entry 5b and draw a face that shows Judy's mood at the end of this chapter. Remind them to look back in their book, if needed.

① SOUND REVIEW

Have students read the sounds. Work for accuracy, then fluency.

② ACCURACY AND FLUENCY BUILDING

- For each task, have students say any underlined part, then read the word.
- Set a pace. Then have students read the whole words in each task and column.
- Provide repeated practice, building accuracy first, then fluency.

E1. Tricky Words

- For each Tricky Word, have students use the sounds and word parts they know to silently sound out the word. Use the word in a sentence to help with pronunciation.

remove	The room was so hot that Ruben decided to . . . *remove* . . . his sweater.
gonna	When Hannah asked Trish to jump down the stairs, she said, "No, I'm not . . . *gonna.*"
worse	Taylor had to stay home from school when his cold got . . . *worse.*
cousin	This summer, Josiah is going to visit his favorite . . . *cousin.*

- Have students go back and read the whole words in the column.

③ WORDS IN CONTEXT

For each word, have students use the sounds and word parts they know to silently sound out the word. Then have students read the sentence. Assist, as needed.

④ MULTISYLLABIC WORDS

For each word, have students read the syllables, then the whole word. Use the word in a sentence, as appropriate.

complained	Even though Aisha got everything she wanted, she still . . . *complained.*
gobbled	Oh no! The hot dogs are gone. Someone . . . *gobbled* . . . them up.
container	Please put the leftover salad in the plastic . . . *container.*
stubborn	Once Sheila makes up her mind, she doesn't change it. She's . . . *stubborn.*
emergency	My aunt is a doctor who works in the . . . *emergency* . . . room.
ozone	The Earth is protected from the sun's harmful rays by . . . *ozone.*

⑤ MORPHOGRAPHS AND AFFIXES

- Have students read the underlined part, then the whole word.
- Review the morphograph *-ful,* as time allows. Say something like:
  Put your finger on the next word. Read the underlined part, then the word. (ful, harmful)
  What does *-ful* mean? (full of) Right, so *harmful* means . . . full of harm.

- Repeat practice with whole words, mixing group and individual turns.
  Build accuracy, then fluency.

⑥ GENERALIZATION: READING NEW WORDS IN PARAGRAPHS

- Have students read the paragraph silently, then out loud. Tell students to use the sounds and word parts they know to read any difficult words.
- Repeat practice, as needed.

Judy Moody Saves the World!

Unit 24 Exercise 6
Use before Chapter 6

1. SOUND REVIEW Have students review sounds for accuracy, then for fluency.

A	au	oy	gi	ew	oi
B	-dge	aw	ue	kn	ge

2. ACCURACY/FLUENCY BUILDING For each column, have students say any underlined part, then read each word. Next, have them read the column.

A1 Mixed Practice	B1 Mixed Practice	C1 Compound Words	D1 Word Endings	E1 Tricky Words
tigers	yogurt	toadkind	squishy	remove
plopped	hissed	stinkbug	presented	gonna
acid	fault	humankind	bubbles	worse
nudged	scum	leapfrog	blinked	cousin
bloomp	bare	sendoff		
spewed			raise	
			raising	

3. WORDS IN CONTEXT Have students use the sounds they know and then the sentences to pronounce each underlined word.

A	a·quar·i·um	Annie's <u>aquarium</u> has lots of colorful rocks and two goldfish.
B	chor·us	When asked if they wanted recess, the kids said in <u>chorus</u>, "Yeah!"

4. MULTISYLLABIC WORDS Have students read each word part, then read each whole word.

A	com·plained	complained	gob·bled	gobbled
B	con·tain·er	container	stub·born	stubborn
C	e·mer·gen·cy	emergency	o·zone	ozone

5. MORPHOGRAPHS AND AFFIXES Have students read the underlined word part, then the word.

aware<u>ness</u>	harm<u>ful</u>	gent<u>ly</u>	glob<u>al</u>

6. GENERALIZATION Have students read the paragraph silently, then out loud. (New words: Pee Wee, Brad, brainstorm, leapfrog)

The Pee Wee Club met at 2 p.m. Virginia brought snacks—celery sticks and peanut butter—and Brad brought drinks—fruit punch. They met to brainstorm ways to raise money for a trip to the zoo. Then, after the meeting, they played leapfrog. It was a fun day!

46

STORY READING INSTRUCTIONS

Students read Chapter 6 (Pond Scum), pages 64–71 (top two lines) with the teacher and pages 71–77 on their own. Page 71 is split between reading sessions.

COMPREHENSION PROCESSES

Remember, Understand, Apply, Analyze, Evaluate

PROCEDURES

1. Reviewing Chapter 5 (Beetle Emergency)

Summarizing—Solution

Have students turn to page 55. Review the main idea of the chapter. Say something like:

Yesterday you read Chapter 5.

At the beginning of the chapter, Judy couldn't find any information about her beetle. How did Frank help her solve her problem?

(Frank showed her a stamp from his collection that had the beetle on it. His stamp album had information about the beetle.)

2. Introducing Chapter 6 (Pond Scum)

Identifying—Title

• Have students turn to page 64 and read the chapter title.

• Ask students what they think of when they read the chapter title, "Pond Scum."

• Think aloud with students about how some words have multiple meanings. Say something like:

Yes, pond scum is the green film of algae that can form on top of still water. We'll have to read the chapter to find out what it means in the story.

3. First Reading

• Ask questions and discuss the story as indicated by the blue text in this guide.

• Mix group and individual turns, independent of your voice.
Have students work toward a group accuracy goal of 0–6 errors.

• After reading the story, practice any difficult words.
Reread the story if students have not reached the accuracy goal.

4. Second Reading, Timed Readings: Repeated Reading

• As time allows, have students do Timed Readings while others follow along.

• Time individuals for 30 seconds and encourage each child to work for a personal best.

• Determine words correct per minute. Record student scores.

Pond Scum

Judy worked on her report all weekend. In Science on Monday, the class presented its endangered species. Frank told the class how a monkeyface mussel got its name. Jessica Finch showed a shiny pigtoe shell that looked like a striped Hershey's Kiss. Judy bragged about the importance of the northeast beach tiger beetle.

"Tiger beetles recycle dead trees and eat tons of harmful insects, so don't step on

64

PG 65

After Reading the First Paragraph on Page 64

❶ **Evaluate:** Viewing, Responding; **Apply:** Using Vocabulary—endangered
Look at the pictures of the endangered animals on page 65. Which one would you want to learn more about? Why?
(I'd like to learn about the bald eagle because I saw one last summer. I'd like to learn about the shiny pigtoe because I think it has a funny name . . .)

After Reading Page 66

❶ **Understand:** Summarizing—Facts;
Using Vocabulary—recycle
Name three facts you learned about Judy's animal,
the northeast beach tiger beetle.
(They recycle dead trees and eat insects. They
make a loud buzzing sound. They are very fast
and tricky.)

❷ **Apply:** Inferring; Explaining; Using Vocabulary—
habitat
Mr. Todd told the class not to remove creatures
from their natural habitat. Why do you think it's
important to leave creatures in their habitats?
(They might die if you take them out of
their habitat.)

❸ **Apply:** Predicting; Using Vocabulary—creature
What do you think Judy's sudden idea is?
(Judy is going to find some creatures to put back
into the wild.)

After Reading Page 67

❶ **Apply:** Inferring; Using Vocabulary—brilliant
Judy called her idea an *Einstein* idea. Einstein was a
brilliant scientist, so what do you think an Einstein
idea is?
(It's a smart idea. It's a brilliant idea . . .)

After Reading Page 68

❶ **Understand:** Explaining, Using Vocabulary—
mascot
What is Toady?
(Toady is a toad. Toady is the club mascot.)

❷ **Analyze:** Drawing Conclusions; **Apply:** Using
Vocabulary—habitat
Do we know what Judy's great idea is yet? Do you
have any clues?
(They want to get rid of Stink and keep an eye
on Toady. Maybe they are going to do something
to Toady. Maybe they will put Toady back in
his habitat.)

After Reading Page 69

❶ Remember: Identifying—What; **Understand:**
Defining and Using Vocabulary—ignore
When Judy said you could add three letters to
Stink's name to get Stinkbug, what did Stink do?
(He ignored her.)
What does that mean?
(He paid no attention to her.)

After Reading Pages 70 and 71 (top two lines)

❶ Analyze: Drawing Conclusions
Why do you think it was Toady's lucky day?
(The kids are going to put Toady back where
he belongs.)

❷ Analyze: Drawing Conclusions; **Apply:**
Using Idioms and Expressions—get rid of
Why do you think the kids wanted to get rid
of Stink?
(Stink won't want them to put Toady back in the
pond. He will try to stop them.)

STORY READING INSTRUCTIONS

Students read Chapter 6 (Pond Scum), pages 71 (from third line) through 77 without the teacher, independently or with partners.

COMPREHENSION PROCESSES

Understand, Apply

PROCEDURES FOR READING ON YOUR OWN

1. Getting Ready

Have students turn to page 71 and find the third line.

2. Setting a Purpose

Explaining, Inferring

Before students begin reading, say something like:

Now you'll read on your own. Some questions for you to think about are on the board.

- Why was the chapter called "Pond Scum"?
- What was Judy's Einstein idea?
- Why did she think it was a good idea?
- How did Stink feel about her idea?

> **PREP NOTE**
> **Setting a Purpose**
> Write questions on a chalkboard, white board, or large piece of paper before working with your small group.

3. Reading on Your Own: Partner or Whisper Reading

- Have students take turns reading every other page with a partner or have students whisper read pages 71–77 on their own.
- Continue having students track each word with their fingers.

4. Comprehension and Skill Work

Tell students that after they read on their own, they will do Comprehension and Skill Activity 6, write a letter to Judy Moody, and do the Many Faces of Judy Moody for this chapter. Guide practice, as needed. (For teacher directions, see pages 81–83.)

5. Homework 6: New Passage

PG **72**

MAZE READING AND STORY COMPREHENSION

COMPREHENSION PROCESSES

Understand

WRITING TRAITS

Presentation

Comprehension Monitoring
Test Taking

Explaining

Identifying—What
Using Vocabulary—mood

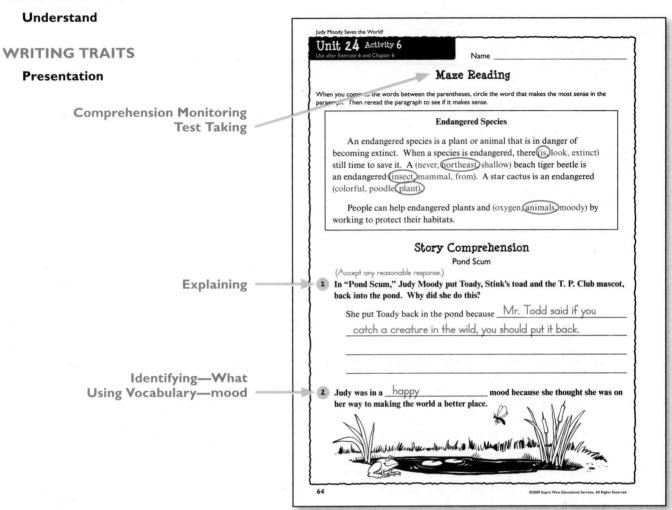

Judy Moody Saves the World!

Unit 24 Activity 6
Use after Exercise 6 and Chapter 6

Name _____

Maze Reading

When you come to the words between the parentheses, circle the word that makes the most sense in the paragraph. Then reread the paragraph to see if it makes sense.

Endangered Species

An endangered species is a plant or animal that is in danger of becoming extinct. When a species is endangered, there (is, look, extinct) still time to save it. A (never, northeast, shallow) beach tiger beetle is an endangered (insect, mammal, from). A star cactus is an endangered (colorful, poodle, plant).

People can help endangered plants and (oxygen, animals, moody) by working to protect their habitats.

Story Comprehension
Pond Scum

(Accept any reasonable response.)

1 In "Pond Scum," Judy Moody put Toady, Stink's toad and the T. P. Club mascot, back into the pond. Why did she do this?

She put Toady back in the pond because __Mr. Todd said if you__
__catch a creature in the wild, you should put it back.__
_____
_____

2 Judy was in a __happy_____ mood because she thought she was on her way to making the world a better place.

64

©2009 Sopris West Educational Services. All Rights Reserved.

PROCEDURES

For each step, demonstrate and guide practice, as needed. Then have students complete the page independently.

Maze Reading—Basic Instructions

Have students read the paragraphs and select the word in the parentheses that best completes each sentence.

Story Comprehension: Sentence Completion—Specific Instructions (Items 1, 2)

Have students read the directions and the sentence starter, then complete the sentence. Remind students to look back in their storybooks. Remind them to end their sentence with a period.

Self-monitoring

Have students check and correct their work.

ENTRIES 6a, 6b

COMPREHENSION PROCESSES
Understand, Apply, Evaluate, Create

WRITING TRAITS
Ideas and Content
Word Choice
Conventions—Complete Sentence, Capital, Period
Presentation

> **SPECIAL NOTE**
> Your students will complete a Dear Judy Moody book. For ease of use, pull pages 47–58 from *Activity Book 4*. Staple the pages together into a book.

PROCEDURES
Have students complete the page independently. Guide practice, only as needed.

Letter Writing: Creative Writing—Specific Instructions (Entry 6a)
- Have students fill in the blanks to complete a letter to Judy Moody.
  Remind them to start sentences with a capital and end with a period.
- Have students draw a picture of Toady in the box at the bottom. Tell them to illustrate how they think Toady feels about being set free.

Cover: Illustrating—Specific Instructions (Entry 6b)
Have students find the box labeled Entry 6b on the cover and draw a face that shows Judy's mood at the end of this chapter. Remind them to look back in their book, if needed.

Generating Ideas
Responding
Sentence
Completion
Sentence Writing

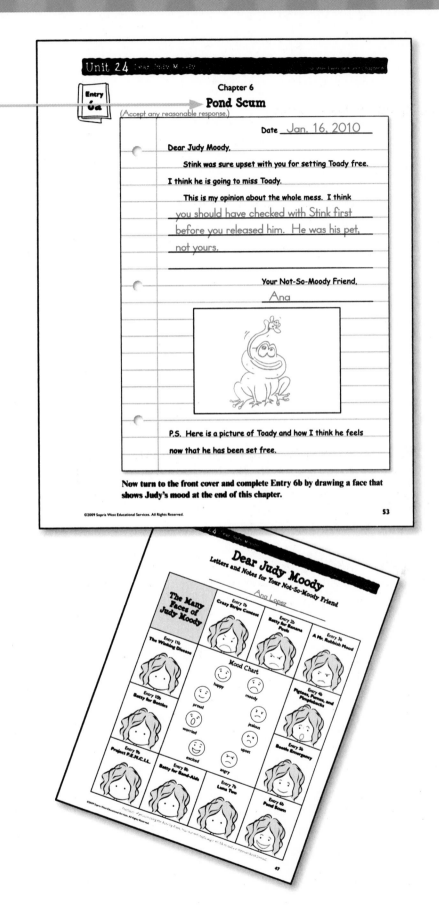

Unit 24 Dear Judy Moody

Entry 6a

Chapter 6

Pond Scum

(Accept any reasonable response.)

Date __Jan. 16, 2010__

Dear Judy Moody,

Stink was sure upset with you for setting Toady free.
I think he is going to miss Toady.

This is my opinion about the whole mess. I think
you should have checked with Stink first
before you released him. He was his pet,
not yours.

Your Not-So-Moody Friend,
Ana

P.S. Here is a picture of Toady and how I think he feels
now that he has been set free.

Now turn to the front cover and complete Entry 6b by drawing a face that
shows Judy's mood at the end of this chapter.

©2009 Sopris West Educational Services. All Rights Reserved.   53

Dear Judy Moody
Letters and Notes for Your Not-So-Moody Friend

Ana Lopez

The Many Faces of Judy Moody

Mood Chart

47

❶ SOUND REVIEW

❷ ACCURACY AND FLUENCY BUILDING

B1. Word Endings

Have students read any underlined word, then the word with an ending.
Use words in sentences, as needed.

baring   When you uncover something, you bare it. Judy is . . . *baring* . . . her teeth.

wailed   When Mom took Baby Jack's bottle of milk away, he . . . *wailed.*

C1. Reading by Analogy

Have students figure out how to read *-cious* by reading other words they know. Use the
words in sentences, as needed.

spacious   The apartment was really roomy. It was . . . *spacious.*

E1. Tricky Words

- For each Tricky Word, have students use the sounds and word parts they know to
  silently sound out the word. Use the word in a sentence to help with pronunciation.
- If the word is unfamiliar, tell students the word.

agua

Look at the first word. The word is *agua*. Say the word. (agua)
Agua is the Spanish word for water. I would really like a little . . . *agua.*
Read the word two times. (agua, agua)

lawsuits

Look at the next word. What small word do you already know? (suits)
Right. Read the word. (lawsuits) When people go to court to settle problems, they have
their lawyers file . . . *lawsuits.* Read the word two times. (lawsuits, lawsuits)

monarch

Look at the next word. The <u>c-h</u> in this word sounds like /k/. Read the word. (monarch)
Someone who rules a kingdom is called a . . . *monarch.* It's also the name of a butterfly.
Read the word two times. (monarch, monarch)

leopard   At the zoo, Maya's class saw a . . . *leopard.*

schedule   Nell needed to go shopping, but couldn't fit it into her . . . *schedule.*

ancient   Grandpa went to Europe and saw castles that were . . . *ancient.*

prey   Predators are hunters. They hunt for . . . *prey.*

- Have students go back and read the whole words in the column.

❸ MULTISYLLABIC WORDS

For each word, have students read the syllables, then the whole word. Use the word in a
sentence, as appropriate.

lentils   For dinner, we had some delicious beans called . . . *lentils.*

appointment   When you have a toothache, you should make a dental . . . *appointment.*

swallowtail   Have you ever seen a butterfly called a . . . *swallowtail?*

lunatic   Angel was acting crazy. She was acting like a . . . *lunatic.*

❹ NAMES AND PLACES

❺ WORDS IN CONTEXT

⑥ **GENERALIZATION: READING NEW WORDS IN PARAGRAPHS**

- Have students read the paragraph silently, then out loud. Tell students to use the sounds and word parts they know to read any difficult words.
- Repeat practice, as needed.

Judy Moody Saves the World!

Unit 24 Exercise 7
Use before Chapter 7

1. SOUND REVIEW Use selected Sound Cards from Units 1–19.

2. ACCURACY/FLUENCY BUILDING For each column, have students say any underlined part, then read each word. Next, have them read the column.

A1 Mixed Practice	**B1** Word Endings	**C1** Reading by Analogy	**D1** Multisyllabic Words	**E1** Tricky Words
c<u>e</u>nts	believe	deli<u>cious</u>	congratulations	agua
tra<u>it</u>or	believing	precious	punishment	lawsuits
envel<u>o</u>pe		spacious	lonely	monarch
styl<u>e</u>	bare		operation	leopard
thi<u>r</u>sty	baring			schedule
ann<u>oy</u>				ancient
	wail			prey
	wailed			

3. MULTISYLLABIC WORDS Have students read each word part, then read each whole word.

Ⓐ	len•tils	lentils	ap•point•ment	appointment
Ⓑ	swal•low•tail	swallowtail	lu•na•tic	lunatic

4. NAMES AND PLACES Have students use the sounds and word parts they know to figure out the words.

Luna Two	Brazil	California	Social Studies

5. WORDS IN CONTEXT Have students use the sounds and word parts they know to figure out each word. Then have them read each sentence.

Ⓐ	Ph.D.	Matt received a <u>Ph.D.</u> after years of college and hard work.
Ⓑ	so•lar•pow•ered	When Todd grows up, he wants to invent a <u>solar-powered</u> car.

6. GENERALIZATION Have students read the paragraph silently, then out loud. (New words: Julia, disagreement, bother, walkie-talkies)

My sister Julia and I had a disagreement about how tall the Empire State Building is. She kept going on and on and finally I said, "Don't bother me!" I went to the tree house to get away from her, but then she called me on our walkie-talkies. I just ignored her.

47

APPROPRIATE CORRECTIONS
(Reminder)

Write any difficult words on a board or clipboard.

Single-Syllable Pattern Words
Have students identify the difficult sound, then sound out and say the word.

Multisyllabic Words
Draw loops under each word part and then guide practice with your hand.

Tricky Words
Have students sound out or read the word by parts, then say the word. Next have students say, spell, and say the word.

After gently correcting a word with the group, go on to other tasks or words. Return to the difficult word at least three times.

COMPREHENSION PROCESSES

Understand, Apply

PROCEDURES

Introducing Vocabulary

> ancient ☆ annoy ☆ budge ☆ traitor ☆ fall for

- For each vocabulary word, have students read the word by parts, then read the whole word.
- Read the student-friendly explanations to students as they follow with their fingers. Then have students use the vocabulary word by following the gray text.
- Review and discuss the illustrations.

  Note: Student vocabulary pages for this unit are found in the students' *Exercise Book 4*.

USING VOCABULARY

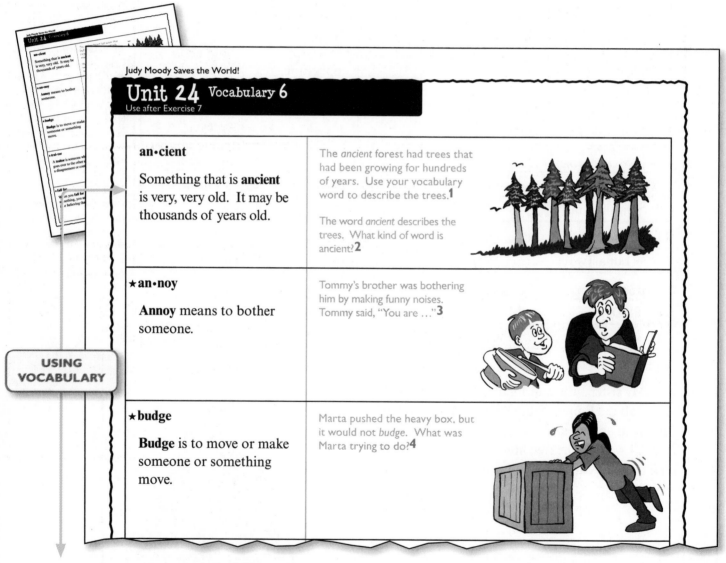

Judy Moody Saves the World!

Unit 24 Vocabulary 6
Use after Exercise 7

an·cient Something that is **ancient** is very, very old. It may be thousands of years old.	The *ancient* forest had trees that had been growing for hundreds of years. Use your vocabulary word to describe the trees.**1** The word *ancient* describes the trees. What kind of word is ancient?**2**
★an·noy **Annoy** means to bother someone.	Tommy's brother was bothering him by making funny noises. Tommy said, "You are …"**3**
★budge **Budge** is to move or make someone or something move.	Marta pushed the heavy box, but it would not *budge*. What was Marta trying to do?**4**

❶ **Apply:** Using Vocabulary—ancient (The trees were ancient.)

❷ **Analyze:** Classifying; **Apply:** Using Vocabulary—ancient (Ancient is an adjective.)

❸ **Apply:** Using Vocabulary—annoy (annoying)

❹ **Apply:** Using Vocabulary—budge (Marta was trying to move the box.)

☆ = New in this unit

USING VOCABULARY

★ **trai·tor**

A **traitor** is someone who goes over to the other side of a disagreement or contest.

When Ben joined another team and played against us, our team felt that he was a ...**1**

★ **fall for**

When you **fall for** something, you are tricked into believing that it is true.

Grandpa pulled a coin out of Cindy's ear, but she knew it was a trick. She was too smart to ...**2**

48

❶ **Apply:** Using Vocabulary—traitor (traitor)

❷ **Apply:** Using Idioms and Expressions—fall for (fall for it)

USING VOCABULARY

Be enthusiastic about learning new words. Keep a running list of words you would like to use and encourage students to use. Keep the list handy when you are teaching. Put students' names on the board to acknowledge use of a word. Say things like:

[Catherine] used the word *annoy* when she talked about the barking dog. That's a great way to use a new vocabulary word.

STORY READING INSTRUCTIONS

Students read Chapter 7 (Luna Two), pages 78–84 (first two lines) with the teacher and pages 84–94 on their own. Page 84 is split at the divider after the first two lines of text.

COMPREHENSION PROCESSES

Remember, Understand, Apply, Analyze, Evaluate, Create

PROCEDURES

1. Reviewing Chapter 6 (Pond Scum)

Summarizing; Locating Information; Inferring; Making Judgments; Using Vocabulary— habitat, permission

Discuss the questions from Chapter 6, Setting a Purpose, and students' questions.

Say something like:

Yesterday, you read the last part of the chapter on your own. Let's see what you learned. Why was the chapter called "Pond Scum"? Look back on page 75 to find that phrase, if you need to. (Judy said Stink would be pond scum if he kept Toady locked up.)

What was Judy's Einstein idea? (She wanted to set Toady free.)

Why did she think it was a good idea?

(She thought Toady should be with other toads. He would be happier in his natural habitat.)

How did Stink feel about what Judy did?

(He was really mad. He will tell on Judy.)

Do you think her idea was a good one? Why or why not?

(It was a bad idea because she should have asked Stink for permission first. He was the one who took care of Toady. It was a good idea because wild animals should be free . . .)

2. Introducing Chapter 7 (Luna Two)

Identifying—Title

Have students read the chapter title. Say something like:

What's the title of this chapter? (Luna Two)

Let's read the chapter and see if we can figure out why Megan McDonald called the chapter "Luna Two."

3. First Reading

- Ask questions and discuss the story as indicated by the blue text in this guide.
  Have students work toward a group accuracy goal of 0–6 errors.
  Quietly keep track of errors made by all students in the group.
- After reading the story, practice any difficult words.
  Reread the story if students have not reached the accuracy goal.

4. Second Reading, Short Passage Practice: Developing Prosody

- As time allows, have students do Timed Readings while others follow along.
- Time individuals for 30 seconds and encourage each child to work for a personal best.
- Determine words correct per minute. Record student scores.

Luna Two

The next day, Judy came home from school and climbed a tree.

She, Judy Moody, was in Trouble with a capital T. Why was her whole family mad at her for letting a toad go free? She was just doing her part to save the world.

Stink saw her up in the tree. "Hey. No fair! Mom and Dad said you had to go straight to your room!"

78

PG 79

After Reading Pages 78 and 79

❶ **Apply:** Inferring; Using Vocabulary—mood
What kind of mood is Judy in?
(She's probably in a bad mood.)

❷ **Understand:** Viewing, Describing; **Apply:** Inferring;
Using Vocabulary—pout
Look at the picture on p. 79. Describe what's happening in the picture.
(Judy is sitting in a tree. She looks mad. Stink is talking to her . . .)
Judy looks like she is pouting. Why do you think she is pouting?
(She's pouting because she doesn't want to stay in her room. She's upset because she is in trouble for letting Toady go. She probably doesn't think she should be punished for doing a good thing . . .)

After Reading Page 80

❶ Understand: Explaining
Why did Julia Butterfly Hill live in a tree?
(She wanted to keep people from cutting it down.)

❷ Remember: Identifying—How Long
How long did she stay in her tree?
(She lived in the tree for two years.)
That's a long time to live in a tree!

After Reading Page 81

❶ Understand: Explaining
Why did Judy want to live in a tree?
(She wanted to be on TV so people would learn
how important trees are.)

❷ Analyze: Drawing Conclusions
What problems do you think Judy might have living
in the tree?
(She doesn't have any food or water. There is no
bathroom. If she goes to sleep, she might fall out
of the tree . . .)

**After Reading Pages 82–84 (to the swirls at
the top of page 84)**

❶ Remember: Identifying—What
What things did Judy ask Stink to bring to her?
(She asked for a walkie-talkie, flashlight, water,
and lentils.)

❷ Create: Generating Ideas
What else do you think she will need to live in
the tree?
(She will need more food. She will need a blanket
to keep her warm at night . . .)

CHAPTER 7 INSTRUCTIONS

Students read Chapter 7 (Luna Two), pages 84–94 without the teacher, independently or with partners.

COMPREHENSION PROCESSES

Understand

PROCEDURES FOR READING ON YOUR OWN

1. Getting Ready

Have students turn to page 84 and find the first sentence after the divider.

2. Setting a Purpose

Explaining

Before students begin reading, say something like:

Now you'll finish the chapter on your own.

As you read, think about the answers to these questions:

- What did Stink and Rocky do to try to get Judy down from the tree?
- What finally made Judy come down?

3. Reading on Your Own: Partner or Whisper Reading

- Have students take turns reading every other page with a partner or have students whisper read pages 84–94 on their own.
- Continue having students track each word with their fingers.

4. Comprehension and Skill Work

Tell students that after they read on their own, they will do Comprehension and Skill Activity 7, write to Judy, and do the Many Faces of Judy Moody for this chapter. Guide practice, as needed. For teacher directions, see pages 92 and 93.)

5. Homework 7: New Passage

> **PREP NOTE**
> **Setting a Purpose**
> Write questions on a chalkboard, white board, or large piece of paper before working with your small group.

VOCABULARY AND STORY COMPREHENSION

COMPREHENSION PROCESSES

Understand, Apply

WRITING TRAITS

Word Choice
Conventions—Complete Sentence,
Capital, Period
Presentation

Using Vocabulary—
recycle, heal, brag, mascot, ancient,
habitat, ignore, compost, ruin, stubborn,
complicated, adopt

Inferring, Explaining

Using Graphic Organizer; Inferring
Using Vocabulary—mood

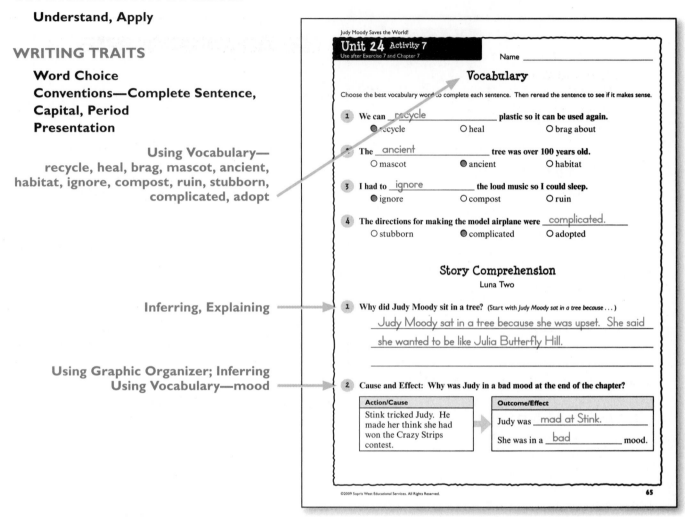

Judy Moody Saves the World!

Unit 24 Activity 7
Use after Exercise 7 and Chapter 7

Name _____

Vocabulary

Choose the best vocabulary word to complete each sentence. Then reread the sentence to see if it makes sense.

1. We can __recycle__ plastic so it can be used again.
   - ● recycle   ○ heal   ○ brag about

2. The __ancient__ tree was over 100 years old.
   - ○ mascot   ● ancient   ○ habitat

3. I had to __ignore__ the loud music so I could sleep.
   - ● ignore   ○ compost   ○ ruin

4. The directions for making the model airplane were __complicated.__
   - ○ stubborn   ● complicated   ○ adopted

Story Comprehension
Luna Two

1. Why did Judy Moody sit in a tree? *(Start with Judy Moody sat in a tree because . . .)*

   Judy Moody sat in a tree because she was upset. She said
   she wanted to be like Julia Butterfly Hill.

2. Cause and Effect: Why was Judy in a bad mood at the end of the chapter?

Action/Cause	Outcome/Effect
Stink tricked Judy. He made her think she had won the Crazy Strips contest.	Judy was __mad at Stink.__ She was in a __bad__ mood.

©2009 Sopris West Educational Services. All Rights Reserved.

65

PROCEDURES

For each step, demonstrate and guide practice, as needed. Then have students complete the
page independently.

Vocabulary: Selection Response—Basic Instructions (Items 1–4)
Have students read each sentence, then fill in the bubble and blank with the correct
vocabulary word. Remind students to put a period at the end of a sentence, where needed.

Story Comprehension

1. Answering Questions: Sentence Writing—Basic Instructions (Item 1)
Have students read the question and write a complete-sentence answer.

2. Cause and Effect: Sequence Chart—Basic Instructions (Item 2)
- Have students read the question and the action/cause sentences.
- Have students explain the outcome by completing the sentences in the second box.

Self-monitoring
Have students read the sentences to see if they make sense.

ENTRIES 7a, 7b

COMPREHENSION PROCESSES

Understand, Apply, Create

WRITING TRAITS

Ideas and Content
Word Choice
Conventions—Question Mark
Presentation

Generating Ideas, Asking Questions
Making Lists, Sentence Completion

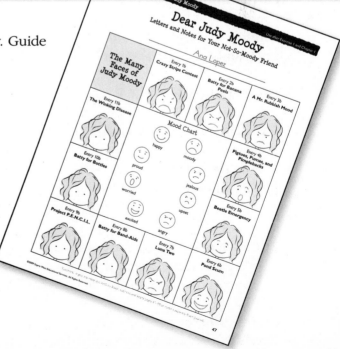

SPECIAL NOTE
Your students will complete a Dear Judy Moody book. For ease of use, pull pages 47–58 from *Activity Book 4*. Staple the pages together into a book.

PROCEDURES

Have students complete the page independently. Guide practice, only as needed.

Letter Writing: Creative Writing—Specific Instructions (Entry 7a)
Have students fill in the blanks to complete a letter to Judy Moody. Remind them to end each question with a question mark.

Cover: Illustrating—Specific Instructions (Entry 7b)
Have students find the box labeled Entry 7b on the cover and draw a face that shows Judy's mood at the end of this chapter. Remind them to look back in their book, if needed.

1 SOUND REVIEW

Have students read the sounds and key word phrases. Work for accuracy, then fluency.

2 ACCURACY AND FLUENCY BUILDING

- For each task, have students say any underlined part, then read the word.
- Set a pace. Then have students read the whole words in each task and column.
- Provide repeated practice, building accuracy first, then fluency.

E1. Tricky Words

- For each Tricky Word, have students use the sounds and word parts they know to silently sound out the word.
  Use the word in a sentence to help with pronunciation.
- If the word is unfamiliar, tell students the word.

casual

Look at the first word. The word is *casual*. Say the word. (casual)
Something that is done without much thought or care is . . . *casual*.
I don't want you to have a *casual* attitude about your homework.
Read the word three times. (casual, casual, casual)

official	The new library opened yesterday. It was the . . . *official* . . . opening.
double	I have twice as much milk as you do. I have . . . *double* . . . the milk.
honorable	She was truthful and had integrity. She was . . . *honorable*.
design	Oh, look at my art project's awesome . . . *design*.

- Have students go back and read the whole words in the column.

3 MULTISYLLABIC WORDS

For each word, have students read the syllables, then the whole word. Use the word in a sentence, as appropriate.

adhesive	We glued the photo to our art project with . . . *adhesive*.
vampires	We read some scary stories about . . . *vampires*.
certificate	Paula didn't miss any school days, so she earned a good attendance . . . *certificate*.
crummy	Freda didn't like her Dad's old car. She thought it was pretty . . . *crummy*.
catalog	Shelley ordered seeds for her garden from the . . . *catalog*.
enclosed	Natasha got a birthday card and found some money . . . *enclosed* . . . within it.

4 WORDS IN CONTEXT

5 GENERALIZATION: READING NEW WORDS IN PARAGRAPHS

- Have students read the paragraph silently, then out loud. Tell students to use the sounds and word parts they know to read any difficult words.
- Repeat practice, as needed.

Judy Moody Saves the World!

Unit 24 Exercise 8
Use before Chapter 8

1. SOUND REVIEW Have students review sounds for accuracy, then for fluency.

A	ow as in snow	u_e as in flute	ph as in phone	oa as in boat	ea as in bread
B	ci	ce	igh	ai	ay

2. ACCURACY/FLUENCY BUILDING For each column, have students say any underlined part, then read each word. Next, have them read the column.

A1 Mixed Practice	B1 Compound Words	C1 Names and Places	D1 Word Endings	E1 Tricky Words
envy	mailbox	October	mistakes	casual
rhino	sunglasses	Josephine	healing	official
supply	rollerblades	Antarctica	cheered	double
fridge	bubble-gum	Mr. Moody	envelopes	honorable
beady		Virginia	jealousy	design

3. MULTISYLLABIC WORDS Have students read each word part, then read each whole word. For Row D, have students read each whole word.

A	ad•he•sive	adhesive	vam•pires	vampires
B	cer•ti•fi•cate	certificate	crum•my	crummy
C	cat•a•log	catalog	en•closed	enclosed
D	mention	decorate	gazillions	ozone

4. WORDS IN CONTEXT Have students use the sounds they know and then the sentences to pronounce each underlined word.

A	bel•fry (bell-free)	A tower with a bell in it is called a belfry.
B	fea•tured	The main act, or featured act, at the show is the clown.
C	CEO	A CEO is the head of a big company.

5. GENERALIZATION Have students read the paragraph silently, then out loud. (New words: Dickson, fame)

When Josh Dickson grows up, he wants to be a doctor. He doesn't want fame and fortune. He also wants to work for good causes. He likes helping people.

49

COMPREHENSION PROCESSES

Apply

PROCEDURES

Introducing Vocabulary

endangered ★ mention ★ original ★ green with envy

- For each vocabulary word, have students read the word by parts, then read the whole word.
- Read the student-friendly explanations to students as they follow with their fingers. Then have students use the vocabulary word by following the gray text.
- Review and discuss the illustrations.

Note: Student vocabulary pages for this unit are found in the students' *Exercise Book 4*.

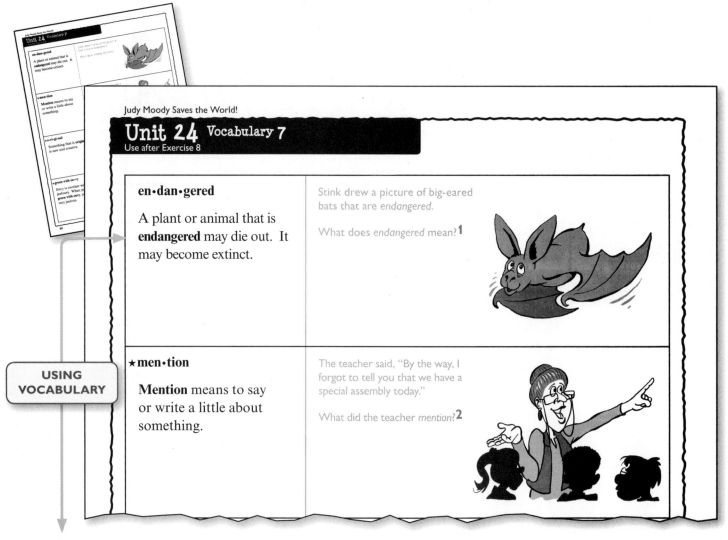

USING VOCABULARY

Judy Moody Saves the World!

Unit 24 Vocabulary 7
Use after Exercise 8

en·dan·gered	Stink drew a picture of big-eared bats that are *endangered*.
A plant or animal that is **endangered** may die out. It may become extinct.	What does *endangered* mean? **1**
★men·tion	The teacher said, "By the way, I forgot to tell you that we have a special assembly today."
Mention means to say or write a little about something.	What did the teacher *mention*? **2**

❶ **Apply:** Using Vocabulary—endangered (The big-eared bats may become extinct.)

❷ **Apply:** Using Vocabulary—mention (The teacher mentioned that there was a special assembly today.)

★ = New in this unit

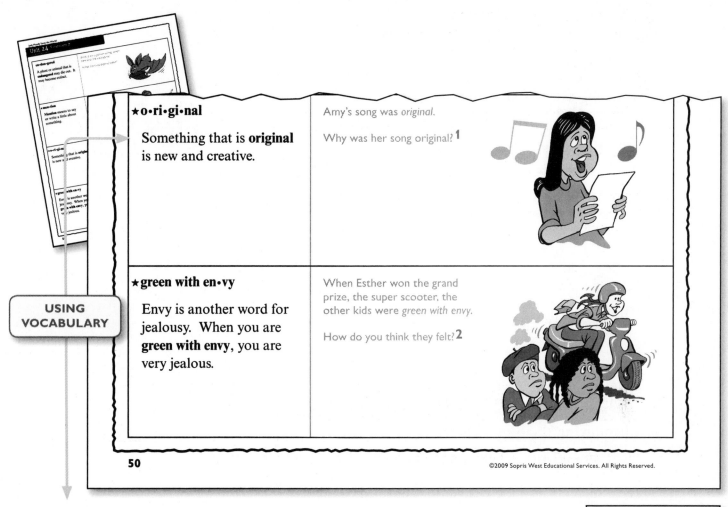

★o•ri•gi•nal

Something that is **original** is new and creative.

Amy's song was *original*.

Why was her song original? **1**

★green with en•vy

Envy is another word for jealousy. When you are **green with envy**, you are very jealous.

When Esther won the grand prize, the super scooter, the other kids were *green with envy*.

How do you think they felt? **2**

USING VOCABULARY

50

❶ **Apply:** Using Vocabulary—original (Amy's song was original because it was new and creative.)

❷ **Apply:** Using Idioms and Expressions—green with envy (The other kids were very jealous.)

USING VOCABULARY

Be enthusiastic about learning new words. Keep a running list of words you would like to use and encourage students to use. Keep the list handy when you are teaching. Put students' names on the board to acknowledge use of a word. Say things like:

[Keiko] used the word *original* when she talked about her brother's artwork. Nice job, [Keiko]!

STORY READING INSTRUCTIONS

Students read Chapter 8 (Batty for Band-Aids), pages 95–100 with the teacher and pages 101–106 on their own.

COMPREHENSION PROCESSES

Remember, Understand, Apply, Create

PROCEDURES

1. **Reviewing Chapter 7 (Luna Two)**

   Summarizing, Inferring

   Discuss the questions from Chapter 7, Setting a Purpose. Say something like:

   Yesterday, you read the last part of the chapter on your own. Let's see what you learned.

   What did Stink and Rocky do to try and get Judy to come out of the tree?
   (They played loud music, they shook the tree, they ignored her . . .)

   What finally made Judy come down?
   (Stink pretended she got a letter from the Crazy Strips Company saying she won the contest.)

   Yes, Stink tricked Judy into coming down from the tree.
   How did that make Judy feel? (Judy was mad.)

2. **Introducing Chapter 8 (Batty for Band-Aids)**

   Identifying—Title; Defining and Using Vocabulary—batty; Inferring; Predicting

   Have students read the chapter title. Say something like:

   Turn to page 95. Read the title of the chapter. (Batty for Band-Aids)
   We've seen the word *batty* before.
   What does batty mean? (Batty means a little crazy.)
   What do you think the chapter title means? (It means crazy for Band-Aids.)
   What do you think this chapter will be about?
   (It will be about the Band-Aids contest . . .)

3. **First Reading**

   • Ask questions and discuss the story as indicated by the blue text in this guide.
   • Mix group and individual turns, independent of your voice.
     Have students work toward a group accuracy goal of 0–6 errors.
   • After reading the story, practice any difficult words.
     Reread the story if students have not reached the accuracy goal.

4. **Second Reading, Timed Readings: Repeated Reading**

   • As time allows, have students do Timed Readings while others follow along.
   • Time individuals for 30 seconds and encourage each child to work for a personal best.
   • Determine words correct per minute. Record student scores.

Batty for Band-Aids

When Judy, Stink, and Rocky got off the bus after school the next day, Stink called, "Race you to the mailbox!" But Judy did not run after Stink. She stayed right where she was so she could watch Rocky do his new disappearing-bubble-gum trick. That's when they heard Stink yell from across the street, "The Crazy Strips Contest! Judy, you won!" He waved an envelope in the air.

95

After Reading Page 95

❶ **Understand:** Explaining
Why didn't Judy run after Stink?
(She wanted to watch Rocky's bubble-gum trick.)

❷ **Understand:** Explaining
Why was Stink excited?
(He thought Judy won the Crazy Strips contest.)

❸ **Apply:** Predicting; Using Vocabulary—theme
Do you think Judy really won the contest?
(Yes, she had a great theme. No, Stink is trying to fool her again.)

PG **97**

After Reading Page 96

❶ **Apply:** Inferring, Explaining
Why wasn't Judy excited when Stink told her the news?
(She thought he was trying to trick her again . . .)

❷ **Apply:** Using Idioms and Expressions—fall for
What's another way to say she won't let him trick her again?
(She won't fall for it.)

After Viewing Page 97

❶ **Apply:** Viewing, Inferring, Explaining
Look at the picture on page 97. What kind of mood is Judy in? Why do you think so?
(She is happy because she got a letter about the contest. She is excited because she thinks she might have won the contest.)

After Reading Page 98

❶ **Understand:** Explaining
What did Judy win?
(She won an honorable mention certificate.)

❷ **Apply:** Inferring, Explaining
How did she feel about her prize?
(She thought it was crummy. She thought she should have won something better.)

After Reading Page 99

❶ Create: Generating Ideas
Rocky tried to cheer Judy up by saying that Stink
hadn't even won a certificate. What would you tell
Judy to cheer her up?
(She can enter again next year. There were
probably lots of really good entries . . .)

❷ Apply: Predicting
What do you think Stink's letter says?
(I think it says he won . . .)

After Reading Page 100

❶ Remember: Identifying—What
What did Stink's Crazy Strips letter say?
(It said he was a winner. It said his design would
be Crazy Strip of the Month.)

❷ Apply: Inferring; Explaining
How did he feel?
(He was happy. He was excited . . .)

❸ Apply: Inferring; **Understand:**
Using Vocabulary—upset, jealous
How did Judy feel?
(She was upset that Stink won a better prize than
she did. She was jealous . . .)

CHAPTER 8 INSTRUCTIONS

Students read pages 101–106 without the teacher, independently or with partners.

COMPREHENSION PROCESSES

Understand, Apply, Create

PROCEDURES FOR READING ON YOUR OWN

1. Getting Ready

Have students turn to page 101.

2. Setting a Purpose

Drawing Conclusions; Defining Idioms and Expressions—green with envy; Making Connections

Establish a purpose for reading. Say something like:

Now you'll read the rest of the chapter on your own to find out what Stink won. As you read, think about Judy's moods and why she feels that way.

As you read the next pages, try to answer these questions:

- At the end of this chapter, Judy was very angry. Why was she angry?
- The author says Judy felt green with envy. What does that mean?
- Has there ever been a time in your life when you were green with envy? If so, why?

PREP NOTE

Setting a Purpose

Write questions on a chalkboard, white board, or large piece of paper before working with your small group.

3. Reading on Your Own: Partner or Whisper Reading

- Have students take turns reading every other page with a partner or have students whisper read pages 101–106 on their own.
- Continue having students track each word with their fingers.

4. Comprehension and Skill Work

Tell students that after they read on their own, they will do Comprehension and Skill Activity 8, write to Judy, and do the Many Faces of Judy Moody for this chapter. Guide practice, as needed. For teacher directions, see pages 103 and 104.

5. Homework 8: New Passage

PG 104

MYSTERY CHARACTER

COMPREHENSION PROCESSES

Understand, Apply

WRITING TRAITS

Word Choice
Conventions—Complete Sentence,
Capital, Period
Presentation

Inferring—Who

Summarizing—Character Traits
(Characterization); Sentence Writing
Illustrating

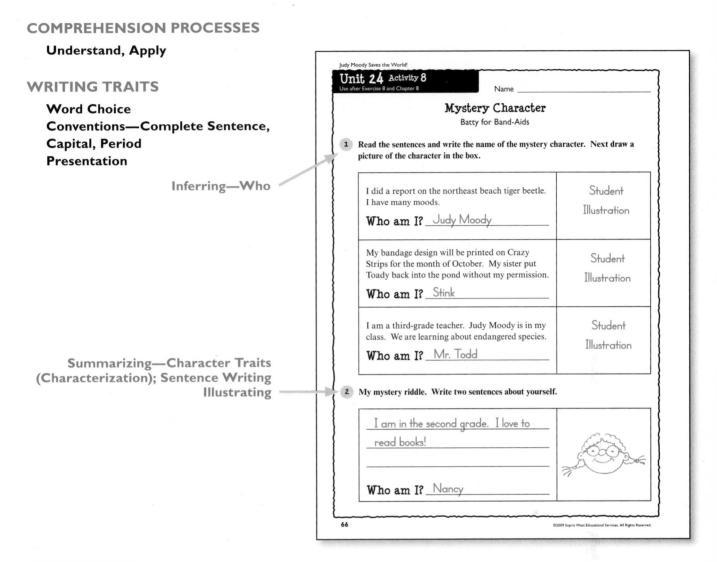

Judy Moody Saves the World!

Unit 24 Activity 8
Use after Exercise 8 and Chapter 8

Name _____

Mystery Character
Batty for Band-Aids

1 Read the sentences and write the name of the mystery character. Next draw a picture of the character in the box.

I did a report on the northeast beach tiger beetle. I have many moods. **Who am I?** _Judy Moody_	Student Illustration
My bandage design will be printed on Crazy Strips for the month of October. My sister put Toady back into the pond without my permission. **Who am I?** _Stink_	Student Illustration
I am a third-grade teacher. Judy Moody is in my class. We are learning about endangered species. **Who am I?** _Mr. Todd_	Student Illustration

2 My mystery riddle. Write two sentences about yourself.

I am in the second grade. I love to read books! **Who am I?** _Nancy_	

66

PROCEDURES

Have students complete the page independently. Guide practice, only as needed.

1. Answering Questions—Specific Instructions
- Have students read the sentence clues, then fill in the blanks with the correct person.
- Have students draw a picture of the character in the box.

2. Self-Characterization: Paragraph Writing—Specific Instructions
- Have students write two sentences about themselves that would help someone else figure out who they are. Have students brainstorm ideas, if needed. Remind them to start sentences with a capital and end with a period.
- Have students draw a self-portrait in the box.

ENTRIES 8a, 8b

COMPREHENSION PROCESSES

Understand, Apply, Evaluate, Create

WRITING TRAITS

Ideas and Content
Word Choice
Conventions—Complete Sentence, Capital, Period
Presentation

SPECIAL NOTE

Your students will complete a Dear Judy Moody book. For ease of use, pull pages 47–58 from *Activity Book 4*. Staple the pages together into a book.

PROCEDURES

Have students complete the page independently. Guide practice, only as needed.

Letter Writing: Creative Writing—Specific Instructions (Entry 8a)
Have students fill in the blanks to complete a letter to Judy Moody.
Encourage them to use at least one of the snazzy vocabulary words listed in the box.
Remind them to start sentences with a capital and end with a period.

Cover: Illustrating—Specific Instructions (Entry 8b)
Have students find the box labeled Entry 8b on the cover and draw a face that shows Judy's mood at the end of this chapter. Remind them to look back in their book, if needed.

Generating Ideas
Responding
Sentence
Completion
Sentence Writing

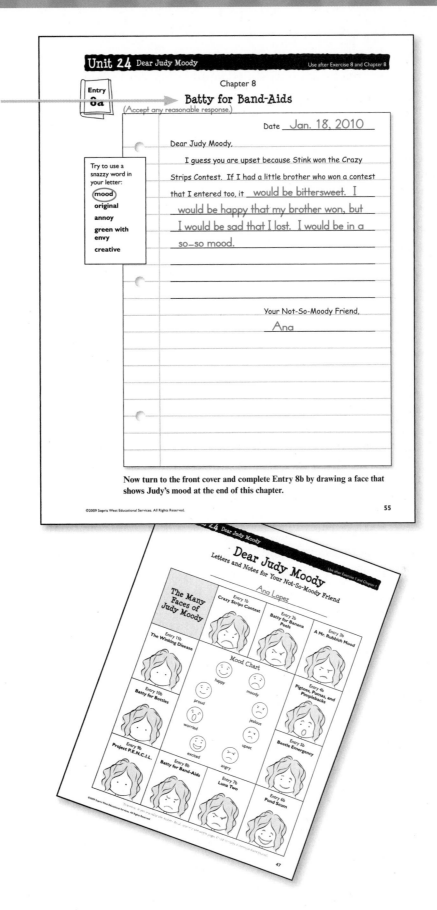

Unit 24 Dear Judy Moody   Use after Exercise 8 and Chapter 8

Entry
8a

Chapter 8

Batty for Band-Aids
(Accept any reasonable response.)

Date **Jan. 18, 2010**

Dear Judy Moody,

I guess you are upset because Stink won the Crazy
Strips Contest. If I had a little brother who won a contest
that I entered too, it **would be bittersweet. I**
would be happy that my brother won, but
I would be sad that I lost. I would be in a
so—so mood.

Your Not-So-Moody Friend,
Ana

Try to use a
snazzy word in
your letter:
mood
original
annoy
green with
envy
creative

Now turn to the front cover and complete Entry 8b by drawing a face that
shows Judy's mood at the end of this chapter.

©2009 Sopris West Educational Services. All Rights Reserved.   55

Dear Judy Moody
Letters and Notes for Your Not-So-Moody Friend

Ana Lopez

The Many
Faces of
Judy Moody

Mood Chart

105

❶ SOUND PRACTICE

- For each task, have students spell and say the focus sound in the gray bar.
- Next, have students read each underlined sound, the word, then the whole column.
- Repeat with each column, building accuracy first, then fluency.

❷ ACCURACY AND FLUENCY BUILDING

- For each task, have students say any underlined part, then read the word.
- Set a pace. Then have students read the whole words in each task and column.
- Provide repeated practice, building accuracy first, then fluency.

B1. Multisyllabic Words

Have students read each whole word. Use each word in a sentence, as needed.

E1. Tricky Words

- For each Tricky Word, have students use the sounds and word parts they know to silently sound out the word. Use the word in a sentence to help with pronunciation.

wash	Our car was dirty, so we took it to the car . . . *wash.*
ecosystem	The Great Barrier Reef has a delicate . . . *ecosystem.*
lovers	The Browns really like dogs. They're dog . . . *lovers.*
neighbors	I live far out in the country, so I don't have any . . . *neighbors.*
thought	Ciara dressed casually. She didn't put a lot of . . . *thought* . . . into it.
through	Finn was careful when he drove . . . *through* . . . the fog.
enough	No more, thank you. I've had . . . *enough.*

- Have students go back and read the whole words in the column.

❸ MULTISYLLABIC WORDS

For each word, have students read the syllables, then the whole word. Use the word in a sentence, as appropriate.

confessed	Jackie admitted to stealing the toy. She . . . *confessed.*
silence	There was no noise, just complete . . . *silence.*
kindergarten	Before you enter first grade, you need to finish . . . *kindergarten.*
promise	When you keep your word, you keep a . . . *promise.*

❹ NAMES AND PLACES

- Tell students these are people and places they will be reading about in the story
- Have students use the sounds and word parts they know to figure out the words. Use the words in sentences, as needed.

❺ WORDS IN CONTEXT

For each word, have students use the sounds and word parts they know to silently sound out the word. Then have students read the sentence. Assist, as needed.

MULTISYLLABIC WORDS CORRECTION PROCEDURE

If students make an error, put the word on the board. Draw loops under each syllable and guide practice with your hand. Have students say each syllable, then read the whole word.

Judy Moody Saves the World!

Unit 24 Exercise 9
Use before Chapter 9

1. SOUND PRACTICE In each column, have students spell and say the sound, next say any underlined sound and the word, then read the column.

gi, ge	ee, ea as in eagle	ci, ce	oa, ow as in snow
ma<u>gi</u>c	p<u>ee</u>ling	pen<u>ci</u>l	t<u>oa</u>d
ori<u>gi</u>nal	fr<u>ea</u>ks	chan<u>ce</u>	rainb<u>ow</u>
banda<u>ge</u>	sn<u>ea</u>ked	<u>ce</u>dar	elb<u>ow</u>

2. ACCURACY/FLUENCY BUILDING For each column, have students say any underlined part, then read each word. Next, have them read the column.

A1 Mixed Practice	B1 Multisyllabic Words	C1 Numbers	D1 Compound Words	E1 Tricky Words
<u>ar</u>my	eraser	twenty	bathtub	wash
f<u>ea</u>ther	acres	thirty	lunchroom	ecosystem
c<u>a</u>st	money	forty	workbooks	lovers
resc<u>ue</u>d	project	fifty	**D2** Related Words	neighbors
v<u>a</u>se	ozone	sixty	grouch	thought
sp<u>e</u>nt	complaining	seventy	grouchy	through
adopt	pretended	eighty	grouchier	enough
		ninety		

3. MULTISYLLABIC WORDS Have students read each word part, then read each whole word.

Ⓐ con·fessed	confessed	si·lence	silence
Ⓑ kin·der·gar·ten	kindergarten	pro·mise	promise

4. NAMES AND PLACES Have students use the sounds and word parts they know to figure out the words.

Ran<u>ge</u>r Rick magazine	Virginia Dare School	Pen<u>ci</u>lvania	Lucy

5. WORDS IN CONTEXT Have students use the sounds and word parts they know to figure out each word. Then have them read each sentence.

Ⓐ chrys·a·lis	A beautiful butterfly emerged from the <u>chrysalis</u>.
Ⓑ caf·e·ter·i·a	The school kids eat lunch in the <u>cafeteria</u>.

ENTHUSIASM

Make a special effort to acknowledge what students can do.

Say things like:
You can read multisyllabic words without help from adults.

You can figure out words you've never seen before.

You can read and use snazzy words like: *neighbors, confessed,* and *ecosystem* . . . That is very impressive.

51

COMPREHENSION PROCESSES
Apply

PROCEDURES
Introducing Vocabulary

☆uproar ☆confess ☆stick your neck out ☆settled, ecosystem

- For each vocabulary word, have students read the word by parts, then read the whole word.
- Read the student-friendly explanations to students as they follow with their fingers. Then have students use the vocabulary word by following the gray text.
- Review and discuss the illustrations.
  Note: Student vocabulary pages for this unit are found in the students' *Exercise Book 4*.

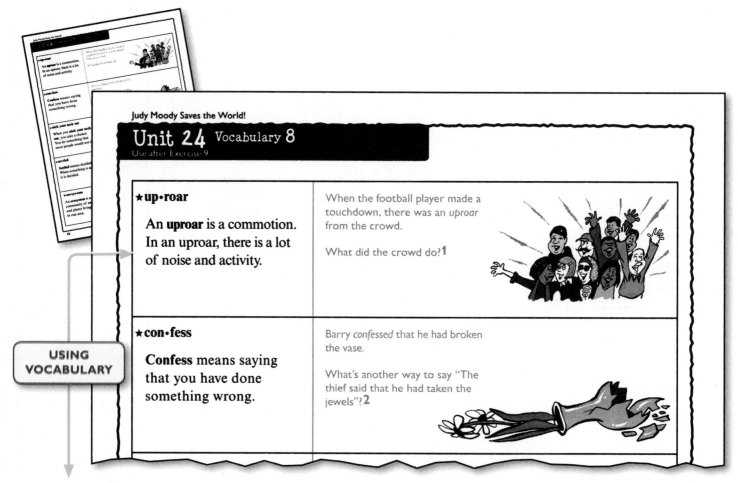

USING VOCABULARY

Judy Moody Saves the World!

Unit 24 Vocabulary 8
Use after Exercise 9

★up•roar

An **uproar** is a commotion. In an uproar, there is a lot of noise and activity.

When the football player made a touchdown, there was an *uproar* from the crowd.

What did the crowd do?**1**

★con•fess

Confess means saying that you have done something wrong.

Barry *confessed* that he had broken the vase.

What's another way to say "The thief said that he had taken the jewels"?**2**

❶ **Apply:** Using Vocabulary—uproar (The crowd made a lot of noise.)

❷ **Apply:** Using Vocabulary—confess (The thief confessed that he had taken the jewels.)

★ = New in this unit

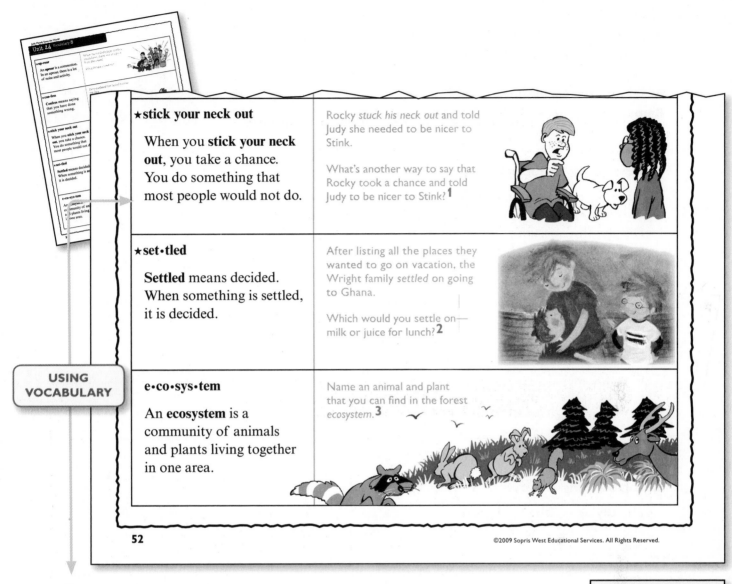

USING VOCABULARY

★**stick your neck out**

When you **stick your neck out**, you take a chance. You do something that most people would not do.

Rocky *stuck his neck out* and told Judy she needed to be nicer to Stink.

What's another way to say that Rocky took a chance and told Judy to be nicer to Stink?**1**

★**set·tled**

Settled means decided. When something is settled, it is decided.

After listing all the places they wanted to go on vacation, the Wright family *settled* on going to Ghana.

Which would you settle on—milk or juice for lunch?**2**

e·co·sys·tem

An **ecosystem** is a community of animals and plants living together in one area.

Name an animal and plant that you can find in the forest *ecosystem.***3**

52

❶ **Apply:** Using Idioms and Expressions—stick your neck out (Rocky stuck his neck out.)

❷ **Apply:** Using Vocabulary—settled (I would settle on juice for lunch.)

❸ **Apply:** Using Vocabulary—ecosystem (You can find a raccoon and a tree in the forest ecosystem.)

USING VOCABULARY

Be enthusiastic about learning new words. Keep a running list of words you would like to use and encourage students to use. Keep the list handy when you are teaching. Put students' names on the board to acknowledge use of a word. Say things like:

[Ned] used the word *uproar* when he described how the dog got loose and ran through the cafeteria. What a great way to use a vocabulary word!

STORY READING INSTRUCTIONS

Students read Chapter 9 (Project P.E.N.C.I.L.), pages 107–113 with the teacher and pages 114–121 on their own.

COMPREHENSION PROCESSES

Remember, Understand, Apply, Analyze, Evaluate

PROCEDURES

1. **Reviewing Chapter 8 (Batty for Band-Aids)**

   Summarizing; Inferring; Defining and/or Using Idioms and Expressions and Vocabulary—jealous, green with envy; Making Connections

   Discuss the questions from Chapter 8, and students' questions. Say something like:

   Yesterday, you read the last part of the chapter on your own. Let's see what you learned.

   At the end of the chapter, Judy was very angry. Why?

   (Stink won sunglasses and 10 boxes of Crazy Strips with his design on it. She was upset and jealous because Stink won and she didn't.)

   The author says Judy felt green with envy. What does that mean?

   (She was very jealous of Stink. She was so jealous she was almost green!)

   Has there ever been a time in your life when you were green with envy? If so, why?

   (I was very jealous when my sister got a brand-new bike. I was green with envy when my brother got to go to the . . .)

2. **Introducing Chapter 9 (Project P.E.N.C.I.L)**

   Identifying—Title; Predicting

   Have students read the chapter title. Say something like:

   Turn to page 107. Read the title of the chapter. (Project P.E.N.C.I.L.)

   What do you think this chapter will be about? (pencils)

3. **First Reading**
   - Ask questions and discuss the story as indicated by the blue text in this guide.
   - Mix group and individual turns, independent of your voice.
     Have students work toward a group accuracy goal of 0–6 errors.
     Quietly keep track of errors made by all students in the group.
   - After reading the story, practice any difficult words.
     Reread the story if students have not reached the accuracy goal.

4. **Second Reading, Short Passage Practice: Developing Prosody**
   - Demonstrate expressive, fluent reading of the first paragraph.
   - Guide practice with your voice.
   - Provide individual turns while others track with their fingers and whisper read.
   - Repeat with one paragraph or page at a time, as time allows.

Project P.E.N.C.I.L.

The next morning, and the next one after that, Judy woke up feeling like a sloth moth. She could hardly make herself get out of bed.

Saving the world was not going so well. She hadn't done anything *really* important. Like heal the world with her own Crazy Strip. So far, she had only saved four banana peels, a lunch bag, and a toad.

107

After Reading Page 107

❶ **Apply:** Inferring, Explaining; Using Vocabulary—discouraged
Why do you think Judy had a hard time getting out of bed for a few days?
(She was discouraged. Saving the world was not going well.)

❷ **Apply:** Inferring, Explaining; **Understand:** Using Vocabulary—mood
What kind of mood is she in?
(She is in a bad mood.)

After Reading Page 108

❶ **Apply:** Inferring, Explaining; **Understand:** Using
Vocabulary—mood, ignore; Viewing
Is Judy still in a bad mood? How can you tell?
(She looks grumpy in the picture. She ate
breakfast in silence. She ignored Stink . . .)

After Reading Pages 109 and 110

❶ **Understand:** Explaining
Why is the rain forest important?
(We depend on the rain forest for things we
eat and use every day. Many animals live in the
rain forest.)

❷ **Remember:** Identifying—Facts; Using
Vocabulary—destroy
What facts about the rain forest did Judy's
class learn?
(In one minute, 100 acres of trees in the rain
forest are destroyed. The wood and rubber used
for pencils comes from the rain forest.)

After Reading Page 111

❶ **Understand:** Explaining
What was Judy's new plan to save the world?
(She took all the pencils and hid them.)

After Reading Page 112

❶ **Analyze:** Drawing Conclusions
Why did she think taking all the pencils was a
good idea?
(She thought if people didn't use pencils, fewer
rain forest trees would be cut down.)

❷ **Evaluate:** Making Judgments; **Analyze:** Drawing
Conclusions
Do you think it was a good idea? Why or not?
(Yes, it will help save some trees, and the class will
have to find a different way to do math. No, the
pencils were already made from the trees, so they
will just go to waste if the kids can't use them.)

STORY READING INSTRUCTIONS

Students read Chapter 9 (Project P.E.N.C.I.L.), pages 114–121 without the teacher, independently or with partners.

COMPREHENSION PROCESSES

Understand, Apply, Create

PROCEDURES FOR READING ON YOUR OWN

1. Getting Ready

Have students turn to page 114.

2. Setting a Purpose

Inferring; Explaining—Solution

Before students begin reading, say something like:

As you read the next pages, try to answer this question:

The kids were mad at Judy. By the end of the chapter, everyone was happy. Why?

3. Reading on Your Own: Partner or Whisper Reading

- Have students take turns reading every other page with a partner or have students whisper read pages 114–121 on their own.

- Continue to have students track each word with their fingers.

4. Comprehension and Skill Work

Tell students that they will do Comprehension and Skill Activity 9, write a letter to Judy Moody, and do the Many Faces of Judy Moody for this chapter. Guide practice, as needed. For teacher directions, see pages 114 and 115.

5. Homework 9: New Passage

> **PREP NOTE**
>
> **Setting a Purpose**
>
> Write questions on a chalkboard, white board, or large piece of paper before working with your small group.

PG **113**

SNAZZY WORDS AND SYNONYMS

STORY COMPREHENSION AND SNAZZY WORDS

COMPREHENSION PROCESSES

Understand, Apply, Analyze

Defining and Using Vocabulary—
creative, outrageous, conserve,
confess, imaginative

Using Vocabulary—
outrageous, conserve, creative,
practical, confess, mood

Using Graphic Organizer
Inferring; Explaining—Event

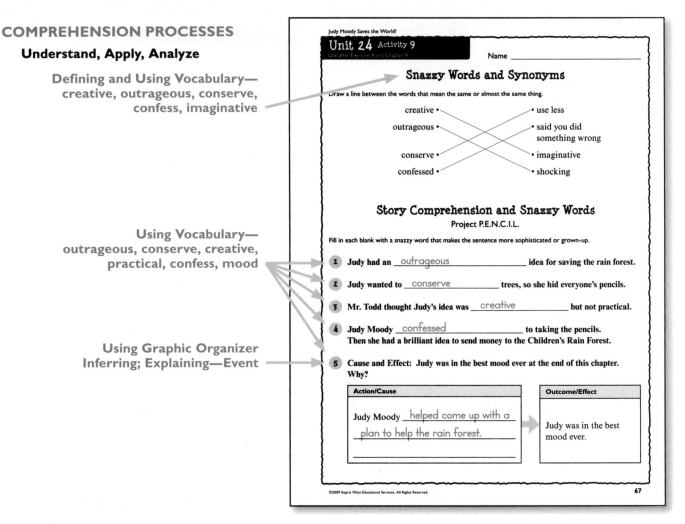

Judy Moody Saves the World!

Unit 24 Activity 9
Use after Exercise 9 and Chapter 9

Name _____

Snazzy Words and Synonyms

Draw a line between the words that mean the same or almost the same thing.

creative •　　　　　　　• use less
outrageous •　　　　　　• said you did something wrong
conserve •　　　　　　　• imaginative
confessed •　　　　　　　• shocking

Story Comprehension and Snazzy Words
Project P.E.N.C.I.L.

Fill in each blank with a snazzy word that makes the sentence more sophisticated or grown-up.

1. Judy had an __outrageous__ idea for saving the rain forest.

2. Judy wanted to __conserve__ trees, so she hid everyone's pencils.

3. Mr. Todd thought Judy's idea was __creative__ but not practical.

4. Judy Moody __confessed__ to taking the pencils. Then she had a brilliant idea to send money to the Children's Rain Forest.

5. Cause and Effect: Judy was in the best mood ever at the end of this chapter. Why?

Action/Cause	Outcome/Effect
Judy Moody __helped come up with a plan to help the rain forest.__ _____	Judy was in the best mood ever.

　67

PROCEDURES

For each step, demonstrate and guide practice, as needed. Then have students complete the page independently.

Snazzy Words and Synonyms, Selection Response—Specific Instructions

Have students read the words in the first column, then choose a word or phrase from the second column that means the same. Have them draw a line between the synonyms.

Story Comprehension and Snazzy Words

1. **Vocabulary: Sentence Completion—Specific Instructions** (Items 1–4)
   Have students read the sentences, then fill in each blank with a vocabulary word from the list at the top of the page.

2. **Cause/Effect: Sequence Chart, Sentence Completion—Specific Instructions** (Item 5)
   Have students read the directions, then write a sentence explaining what Judy did to cause her to be in a good mood.

ENTRIES 9a, 9b

COMPREHENSION PROCESSES

Understand, Apply, Evaluate, Create

WRITING TRAITS

Ideas and Content
Word Choice
Conventions—Complete Sentence,
Capital, Period
Presentation

Generating Ideas, Responding
Sentence Completion; Sentence Writing

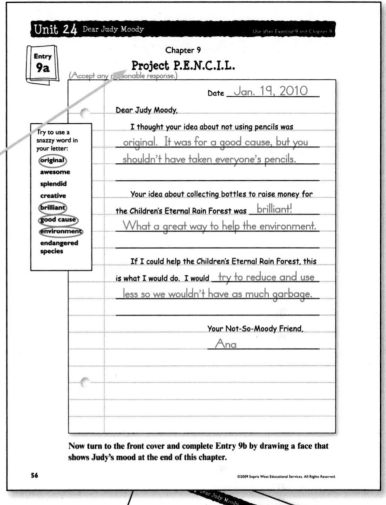

SPECIAL NOTE

Your students will complete a Dear Judy Moody book. For ease of use, pull pages 47–58 from *Activity Book 4*. Staple the pages together into a book.

PROCEDURES

Have students complete the page independently. Guide practice, only as needed.

Letter Writing: Creative Writing—Specific Instructions (Entry 9a)

Have students fill in the blanks to complete a letter to Judy Moody.

Encourage them to use at least one of the snazzy vocabulary words listed in the box.

Remind them to start sentences with a capital and end with a period.

Cover: Illustrating—Specific Instructions (Entry 9b)

Have students find the box labeled Entry 9b on the cover and draw a face that shows Judy's mood at the end of this chapter. Remind them to look back in their book, if needed.

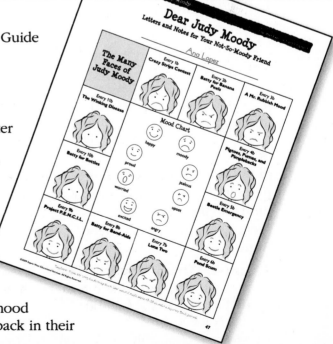

❶ SOUND REVIEW
Use selected Sound Cards from Units 1–19.

❷ SHIFTY WORDS
Have students read the words. Use the words in sentences, as needed.

❸ SOUND PRACTICE
- For each task, have students spell and say the focus sound in the gray bar.
- Next, have students read the whole column.
- Repeat with each column, building accuracy first, then fluency.

❹ ACCURACY AND FLUENCY BUILDING
- For each task, have students say any underlined part, then read the word.
- Set a pace. Then have students read the whole words in each task and column.
- Provide repeated practice, building accuracy first, then fluency.

B1. Related Words
> Tell students these words are all related to "recycle." Have students read each word. Use the words in sentences, as needed.

E1. Tricky Words
- For each Tricky Word, have students use the sounds and word parts they know to silently sound out the word. Use the word in a sentence to help with pronunciation.

  presidential
  Look at the first word. You already know part of this word. What is it? (president) Right, now read the whole word. (presidential) Something that has to do with the president is . . . *presidential.* Read the word two times. (presidential, presidential)

tomorrow's	Tomorrow is a big day. Another way to say that is . . . *tomorrow's* . . . a big day.
wear	Paris wanted to go to the party, but she didn't have anything nice to . . . *wear.*
mountain	I would like to climb a big . . . *mountain.*
country	Brazil is a . . . *country.*

- Have students go back and read the whole words in the column.

❺ MULTISYLLABIC WORDS
For each word, have students read the syllables, then the whole word. Use the word in a sentence, as appropriate.

igloo	An Eskimo lives in a house called an . . . *igloo.*
announcement	The principal said, "I have an important . . . *announcement.*"
principal	Ms. Blancher is our school's . . . *principal.*
multipurpose	Our school gym is used for many things. It's a . . . *multipurpose* . . . room.
total	The grocery clerk added everything up and gave me the . . . *total.*
regular	We don't have a short day at school today. We'll follow our . . . *regular* . . . schedule.

❻ MORPHOGRAPHS AND AFFIXES
- Have students read the underlined part, then the whole word.
- Repeat practice with whole words, mixing group and individual turns. Build accuracy, then fluency.

Judy Moody Saves the World!

Unit 24 Exercise 10
Use before Chapter 10

1. SOUND REVIEW Use selected Sound Cards from Units 1–19.

2. SHIFTY WORDS Have students read the words.

peace	pace	race	trace	trade

3. SOUND PRACTICE In each column, have students spell and say the sound. Next, have students read the whole column.

ph	ea as in bread	au	-dge
trophy	Heather	cause	trudged
Stephanie	leather	Paul	budge
gopher	feather	fault	fridge

4. ACCURACY/FLUENCY BUILDING For each column, have students say any underlined part, then read each word. Next, have them read the column.

A1 Mixed Practice	B1 Related Words	C1 Word Endings	D1 Word Endings	E1 Tricky Words
c<u>oa</u>t	recycle	<u>crush</u>ed	pile	presidential
fr<u>a</u>mes	recycled	<u>raid</u>ed	piling	tomorrow's
st<u>a</u>sh	recycling	<u>stomp</u>s		wear
<u>c</u>ircle		<u>miss</u>es	easy	mountain
ok<u>ay</u>		<u>feed</u>ers	easier	country
gar<u>a</u>ge		<u>hanger</u>s		

5. MULTISYLLABIC WORDS Have students read each word part, then read each whole word.

Ⓐ ig·loo	igloo	an·nounce·ment	announcement
Ⓑ prin·ci·pal	principal	mul·ti·pur·pose	multipurpose
Ⓒ to·tal	total	reg·u·lar	regular

6. MORPHOGRAPHS AND AFFIXES Have students read the underlined word part, then the word.

Ⓐ <u>ex</u>tremely	invis<u>ible</u>	honor<u>able</u>	outrag<u>eous</u>	<u>dis</u>agreement
Ⓑ ero<u>sion</u>	funer<u>al</u>	collec<u>tion</u>	environ<u>ment</u>	pollu<u>tion</u>

53

STORY READING INSTRUCTIONS

Students read Chapter 10 (Batty for Bottles), pages 122–127 with the teacher.

COMPREHENSION PROCESSES

Remember, Understand, Apply, Analyze, Create

PROCEDURES

1. **Reviewing Chapter 9 (Project P.E.N.C.I.L.)**

   Summarizing; Inferring; Using Vocabulary—mood

   Quickly discuss the questions from Chapter 9, Setting a Purpose. Say something like:

   Yesterday you read pages 114–121 on your own. Let's see what you found out.

   The kids were mad at Judy. By the end of the chapter, everyone was happy. Why?

   (The kids decided to raise some money to plant trees in the rain forest. Judy helped come up with the idea. Everyone was in a good mood because they figured out something they could do to help protect the rain forest.)

2. **Introducing Chapter 10 (Batty for Bottles)**

   Identifying—Title; Using Vocabulary—batty; Predicting

   Have students read the chapter title. Say something like:

   Turn to page 122. Read the title of the chapter. (Batty for Bottles)

   There's that word *batty* again.

   What's another way to say the chapter title? (Crazy about Bottles)

   What do you think will happen in this chapter? (The kids will collect lots of bottles.)

3. **First Reading**
   - Ask questions and discuss the story as indicated by the blue text in this guide.
   - Mixing turns, have students work toward a group accuracy goal of 0–6 errors. Quietly keep track of errors made by all students in the group.
   - After reading the story, practice any difficult words.

4. **Second Reading, Short Passage Practice: Developing Prosody**
   - Demonstrate expressive, fluent reading of the first two paragraphs.
   - Guide practice with your voice.
   - Provide individual turns while others track with their fingers and whisper read.
   - Repeat with one paragraph at a time.

5. **Partner or Whisper Reading: Repeated Reading**

   Before independent work, have students finger track and partner or whisper read.

6. **Comprehension and Skill Work**

   Tell students that they will do Comprehension and Skill Activities 10 and 11, write a letter to Judy, and complete the Many Faces of Judy Moody for this chapter. Guide practice, as needed. For teacher directions, see pages 121–123.

7. **Homework 10: New Passage**

Batty for Bottles

"Let's go on a bottle hunt," said Rocky. "After school."

"I sure hope bottles are easier to find than northeast beach tiger beetles," Judy said.

They raided Rocky's garage first and found two milk crates full of bottles that had not been recycled. "Rare!" said Judy. "Twenty-seven bottles!"

122

After Reading Pages 122 and 123

❶ **Understand:** Explaining
What were Rocky and Judy doing?
(They were collecting bottles for the bottle drive.)

❷ **Create:** Generating Ideas; **Apply:**
Using Vocabulary—garbage
If you were collecting bottles, where would you look for them?
(I'd look at the park after a ball game, in people's garages, in garbage cans . . .)

PG **127**

After Reading Page 124

1 **Remember:** Identifying—How Many; **Apply:** Using Vocabulary—garbage; **Analyze:** Drawing Conclusions
According to Mr. Todd, how many plastic bottles do people throw away in three months?
(People throw away enough bottles to circle the whole Earth.)
Why is that a problem?
(That's a lot of bottles that have to go in the trash. We could run out of places to put our garbage. The trash goes in places where animals need to live . . .)

After Reading Page 125

1 **Remember:** Identifying—What; Locating Information
Name three things that can be made from recycled plastic bottles. Look in your book, if you need to.
(You can make clothes, toys, and coat hangers from recycled plastic bottles.)

After Reading Page 126 and Viewing Page 127

1 **Understand:** Viewing, Describing
What does the picture show?
(It shows the kids and lots of bottles.)

2 **Apply:** Inferring, Explaining
Why is tomorrow going to be a big day for the class?
(They will find out how much money they've raised and how many trees will be planted in the rain forest.)

PASSAGE READING FLUENCY

FLUENCY

Accuracy, Expression, Rate

PROCEDURES

For each step, demonstrate and guide practice, as needed. Then have students complete the page independently.

Passage Reading—Basic Instructions

- Have students read the practice words.
- Have students finger track and whisper read the story two times— the first time for accuracy and the second time for expression. Have students cross out an orangutan each time they finish.
- Have students do a one-minute Timed Reading and cross out the timer.

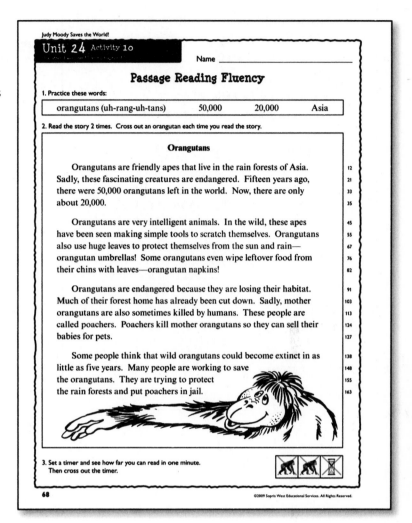

Judy Moody Saves the World!

Unit 24 Activity 10

Name _____

Passage Reading Fluency

1. Practice these words:

orangutans (uh-rang-uh-tans)	50,000	20,000	Asia

2. Read the story 2 times. Cross out an orangutan each time you read the story.

Orangutans

    Orangutans are friendly apes that live in the rain forests of Asia. Sadly, these fascinating creatures are endangered. Fifteen years ago, there were 50,000 orangutans left in the world. Now, there are only about 20,000. — 12, 21, 33, 35

    Orangutans are very intelligent animals. In the wild, these apes have been seen making simple tools to scratch themselves. Orangutans also use huge leaves to protect themselves from the sun and rain— orangutan umbrellas! Some orangutans even wipe leftover food from their chins with leaves—orangutan napkins! — 45, 55, 67, 76, 82

    Orangutans are endangered because they are losing their habitat. Much of their forest home has already been cut down. Sadly, mother orangutans are also sometimes killed by humans. These people are called poachers. Poachers kill mother orangutans so they can sell their babies for pets. — 91, 103, 113, 124, 127

    Some people think that wild orangutans could become extinct in as little as five years. Many people are working to save the orangutans. They are trying to protect the rain forests and put poachers in jail. — 138, 148, 155, 163

3. Set a timer and see how far you can read in one minute. Then cross out the timer.

68

©2009 Sopris West Educational Services. All Rights Reserved.

LOCATING INFORMATION • FACT SUMMARY

COMPREHENSION PROCESSES
Remember, Understand

WRITING TRAITS
Organization—Topic Sentence, Supporting Details
Conventions—Complete Sentence, Capital, Period
Presentation

Using Graphic Organizer
Locating Information; Identifying—
Supporting Details
Using Vocabulary—endangered, habitat

Summarizing—Main Idea/Topic
Supporting Details/Facts
Using Vocabulary—
endangered, habitat, protect
Sentence Writing

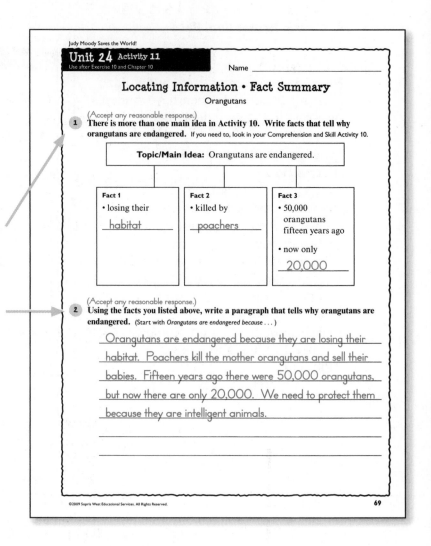

Judy Moody Saves the World!

Unit 24 Activity 11
Use after Exercise 10 and Chapter 10

Name _____

Locating Information • Fact Summary
Orangutans

(Accept any reasonable response.)

1 There is more than one main idea in Activity 10. Write facts that tell why orangutans are endangered. If you need to, look in your Comprehension and Skill Activity 10.

Topic/Main Idea: Orangutans are endangered.

Fact 1
• losing their
  habitat

Fact 2
• killed by
  poachers

Fact 3
• 50,000 orangutans fifteen years ago
• now only
  20,000

(Accept any reasonable response.)

2 Using the facts you listed above, write a paragraph that tells why orangutans are endangered. (Start with *Orangutans are endangered because* . . .)

Orangutans are endangered because they are losing their habitat. Poachers kill the mother orangutans and sell their babies. Fifteen years ago there were 50,000 orangutans, but now there are only 20,000. We need to protect them because they are intelligent animals.

©2009 Sopris West Educational Services. All Rights Reserved. 69

PROCEDURES
For each step, demonstrate and guide practice, as needed. Then have students complete the page independently.

1. **Main Idea/Supporting Details: Hierarchy Chart—Basic Instructions** (Item 1)
   • Have students read the topic/main idea.
   • Have students complete the facts about orangutans.

2. **Fact Summary: Paragraph Writing—Basic Instructions** (Item 2)
   Have students write a fact summary paragraph with the facts from Item 1. Assist, only as needed.

Self-monitoring
Have students check and correct their work.

ENTRIES 10a, 10b

COMPREHENSION PROCESSES
Understand, Apply, Evaluate, Create

WRITING TRAITS
Ideas and Content
Word Choice
Conventions—Period
Presentation

Inferring, Generating Ideas, Responding
Sentence Completion

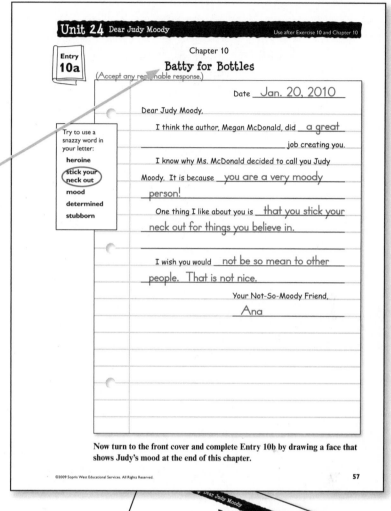

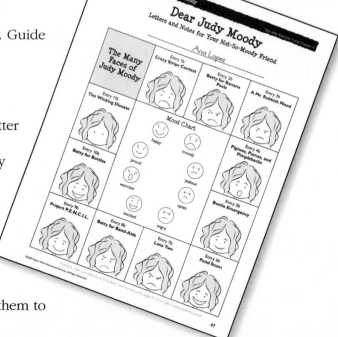

SPECIAL NOTE
Your students will complete a Dear Judy Moody book. For ease of use, pull pages 47–58 from *Activity Book 4*. Staple the pages together into a book.

PROCEDURES
Have students complete the page independently. Guide practice, only as needed.

Letter Writing: Creative Writing—Specific Instructions (Entry 10a)
Have students fill in the blanks to complete a letter to Judy Moody.
Encourage them to use at least one of the snazzy vocabulary words listed in the box.
Remind them to end sentences with a period.

Cover: Illustrating—Specific Instructions (Entry 10b)
Have students find the box labeled Entry 10b on the cover and draw a face that shows Judy's mood at the end of this chapter. Remind them to look back in their book, if needed.

① SHIFTY WORDS

Have students read the words. Use the words in sentences, as needed.

② SOUND PRACTICE

③ ACCURACY AND FLUENCY BUILDING

- For each task, have students say any underlined part, then read the word.
- Set a pace. Then have students read the whole words in each task and column.
- Provide repeated practice, building accuracy first, then fluency.

B1. Contractions

- Prompt students to tell you what a contraction is.
- For each set, have students read the words, then the contraction.

C1. Multisyllabic Words

- For the list of words divided by syllables, have students read each syllable, then the word.
- For the list of whole words, build accuracy and then fluency.

donated	Kevin's family took items they didn't use anymore and . . . *donated* . . . them.
assembly	The school had an . . . *assembly*.
efforts	The principal said, "We really appreciate all your . . . *efforts*."
contribution	The street musician hoped people would give him money, or a . . . *contribution*.
department	The ranger works for the county parks . . . *department*.
absolute	There was no noise at all. There was . . . *absolute* . . . silence.
announcements	We heard about a contest during the school's morning . . . *announcements*.

E1. Tricky Words

- For each Tricky Word, have students use the sounds and word parts they know to silently sound out the word. Use the word in a sentence to help with pronunciation.
- If the word is unfamiliar, tell students the word.

papier mâché
Look at the first word. The word is *papier mâché*. Read the word. (papier mâché) Papier mâché is a French word that means chewed paper. You can make masks and other projects with . . . *papier mâché*. Read the word two times. (papier mâché, papier mâché)

self-portraits
Look at the next word. The word is *self-portraits*. Read the word. (self-portraits)
We drew our own . . . *self-portraits*. Read the word two times. (self-portraits, self-portraits)

appreciation	Mandy took her son swimming so he gave her flowers to show his . . . *appreciation*.
behalf	Dad works hard on his children's . . . *behalf*.
straighter	Dennis got braces to make his teeth . . . *straighter*.
doubt	Ana asked, "Do you think our plan will work?" Jorge said, "I . . . *doubt* . . . it."
meant	Penny didn't understand what her brother . . . *meant*.

- Have students go back and read the whole words in the column.

④ NAMES

SHIFTY WORDS CORRECTION PROCEDURE

If students make an error, put the word on the board. Underline the incorrect sound.

Have students identify the difficult sound, then sound the word out smoothly. Have students read the row again. Return to the difficult word for three correct responses.

⑤ GENERALIZATION: READING NEW WORDS IN PARAGRAPHS
- Have students read the paragraph silently, then out loud. Tell students to use the sounds and word parts they know to read any difficult words.
- Repeat practice, as needed.

Judy Moody Saves the World!

Unit 24 Exercise 11
Use before Chapter 11

1. SHIFTY WORDS Have students read the words.

scoot	shoot	boot	beat	beast

2. SOUND PRACTICE In each column, have students spell and say the sound, next say any underlined sound and the word, then read the column.

ce	gi	**ea** as in eagle	Rhyming Words
ac<u>ce</u>pt	<u>gi</u>raffe	b<u>ea</u>m	winking
chan<u>ce</u>	en<u>gi</u>ne	cr<u>ea</u>m	blinking
con<u>ce</u>rned	Vir<u>gi</u>nia	sp<u>ea</u>k	stinking

3. ACCURACY/FLUENCY BUILDING For each column, have students say any underlined part, then read each word. Next, have them read the column.

A1 Mixed Practice	**B1** Contractions	**C1** Multisyllabic Words		**D1** Tricky Words
s<u>qu</u>int	we would	do•nat•ed	donated	papier mâché
s<u>qu</u>irmed	we'd	as•sem•bly	assembly	self-portraits
sh<u>o</u>ne		ef•forts	efforts	appreciation
c<u>ou</u>nty	how is	con•tri•bu•tion	contribution	behalf
rej<u>oi</u>n	how's	de•part•ment	department	straighter
<u>a</u>bsent		ab•so•lute	absolute	doubt
		an•nounce•ments	announcements	meant

4. NAMES Have students use the sounds and word parts they know to figure out the words.

Screamin' Mimi's	Margaret Mead	Siberian tiger	Ranger Piner

5. GENERALIZATION Have students read the paragraph silently, then out loud. (New words: represent, PA system, kiddo, deserving, positive)

Jessica was so happy. It was just announced over the school PA system that she was going to Washington, D.C., to represent her class at the Students for Change meeting. Her teacher said, "Hey, kiddo, you're very deserving of this honor. I'm positive you'll do a good job."

COMPREHENSION PROCESSES

Apply

PROCEDURES

Introducing Vocabulary

★ **on behalf of** ★ **concerned** ★ **appreciation** ★ **contribution**

- For each vocabulary word, have students read the word by parts, then read the whole word.
- Read the student-friendly explanations to students as they follow with their fingers. Then have students use the vocabulary word by following the gray text.
- Review and discuss the illustrations.
  Note: Student vocabulary pages for this unit are found in the students' *Exercise Book 4.*

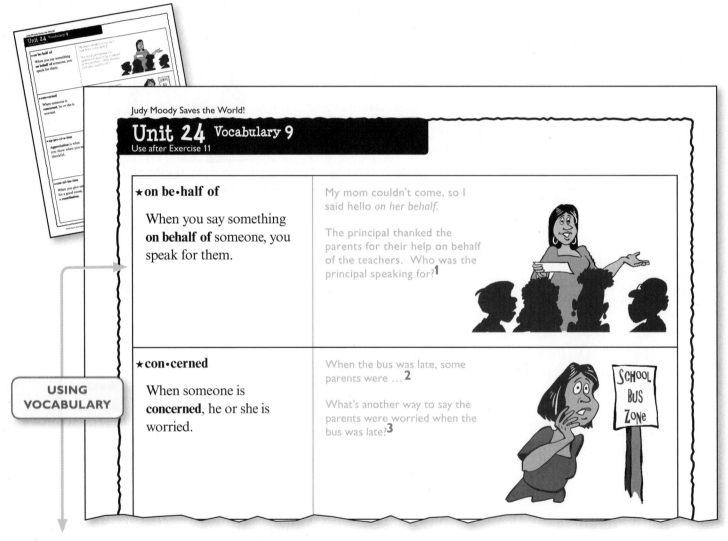

Judy Moody Saves the World!

Unit 24 Vocabulary 9
Use after Exercise 11

★ **on be·half of**

When you say something **on behalf of** someone, you speak for them.

My mom couldn't come, so I said hello *on her behalf.*

The principal thanked the parents for their help on behalf of the teachers. Who was the principal speaking for?[1]

★ **con·cerned**

When someone is **concerned**, he or she is worried.

When the bus was late, some parents were … [2]

What's another way to say the parents were worried when the bus was late?[3]

SCHOOL BUS ZONE

USING VOCABULARY

❶ **Apply:** Using Idioms and Expressions—on behalf of (The principal was speaking for the teachers.)
❷ **Apply:** Using Vocabulary—concerned (concerned)
❸ **Apply:** Using Vocabulary—concerned (The parents were concerned when the bus was late.)

★ = New in this unit

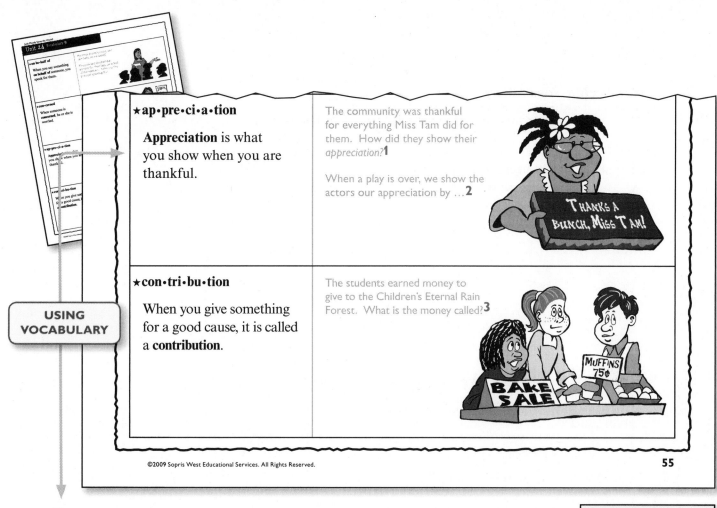

USING VOCABULARY

★**ap•pre•ci•a•tion**

Appreciation is what you show when you are thankful.

The community was thankful for everything Miss Tam did for them. How did they show their *appreciation?***1**

When a play is over, we show the actors our appreciation by ...**2**

THANKS A BUNCH, MISS TAM!

★**con•tri•bu•tion**

When you give something for a good cause, it is called a **contribution**.

The students earned money to give to the Children's Eternal Rain Forest. What is the money called?**3**

BAKE SALE

MUFFINS 75¢

55

❶ **Apply:** Using Vocabulary—appreciation (They had a party for her.)
❷ **Apply:** Using Vocabulary—appreciation (clapping)
❸ **Apply:** Using Vocabulary—contribution (The children's money is a contribution.)

USING VOCABULARY

Be enthusiastic about learning new words. Keep a running list of words you would like to use and encourage students to use. Keep the list handy when you are teaching. Put students' names on the board to acknowledge use of a word. Say things like:

[Ram] used the word *appreciation* when he thanked our classroom volunteers today. What a great way to use a vocabulary word!

STORY READING INSTRUCTIONS

Students read Chapter 11 (The Winking Disease), pages 128–137 with the teacher and pages 138–144 on their own.

COMPREHENSION PROCESSES

Remember, Understand, Apply

PROCEDURES

1. Reviewing Chapter 10 (Batty for Bottles)

Summarizing; Inferring—Main Idea

Have students turn to page 122. Review the main idea of the chapter, then discuss students' questions about Chapter 10. Say something like:

Yesterday you read Chapter 10. What was Judy Moody's class doing?
(They were collecting bottles.)

Why? (They were trying to earn money to plant trees in the rain forest.)

So what was the main idea of the chapter?

(Judy Moody's class was collecting bottles to earn money to plant trees in the rain forest.)

2. Introducing Chapter 11 (The Winking Disease)

Identifying—Title; Inferring

Have students read the chapter title. Say something like:

Turn to page 128. Read the title of the chapter. (The Winking Disease)

What do you think that can mean? (Someone has a problem with winking.)

I guess we'll have to read to find out.

3. First Reading

- Ask questions and discuss the text as indicated by the blue text in this guide.
- Mix group and individual turns, independent of your voice.
  Have students work toward a group accuracy goal of 0–6 errors.
  Quietly keep track of errors made by all students in the group.
- After reading the story, practice any difficult words.
  Reread the story if students have not reached the accuracy goal.

4. Second Reading, Timed Readings: Repeated Reading

- As time allows, have students do Timed Readings while others follow along.
- Time individuals for 30 seconds and encourage each child to work for a personal best.
- Determine words correct per minute. Record student scores.

The Winking Disease

When Judy and Rocky stepped off the bus on Friday morning, Ms. Tuxedo was standing outside the school doors. "How's it going, you two?"

"Pretty good, I guess," said Judy.

"Today we find out how many trees we're going to plant," said Rocky.

"That's right," the principal said. "You both have a good day." And she winked. Judy looked at Rocky. Rocky looked at Judy.

128

After Reading Page 128 and Viewing Page 129

❶ **Apply:** Inferring; Explaining
Why would this be a good day for Judy and her class?
(They will find out how many bottles they collected.)

❷ **Apply:** Viewing, Inferring, Explaining
Look at the picture on page 129. Why do you think Rocky and Judy are looking at each other with puzzled looks?
(Ms. Tuxedo is winking, and they're wondering why she's winking.)

After Reading Page 131

❶ **Remember:** Identifying—Who
Who winked at Rocky and Judy?
(Ms. Tuxedo and Mr. Todd both winked at them.)

❷ **Understand:** Explaining
What is the winking disease?
(It's when people wink at you and say nice things.)

❸ **Apply:** Inferring, Explaining
What did Judy think the winking disease meant?
(She thought something was up.)

After Reading Page 133

❶ **Remember:** Identifying—Where
The kids earned enough to buy 100 trees. Where
will they be planted?
(The trees will be planted in the Children's Rain
Forest in Costa Rica.)

❸ **Apply:** Making Connections, Priming
Background Knowledge
We read about the Children's Rain Forest in our
last unit.
What do you remember about the rain forest?
(It was started by a Swedish boy. The forest is still
growing. Kids from all over the world send money
to buy trees . . .)

After Reading Page 134

❶ **Understand:** Explaining; Using Vocabulary—
summoned
Why was Judy summoned to the front office?
(She will represent the class at the assembly.)

❷ **Apply:** Inferring, Explaining
How did she feel about that?
(She was proud and happy.)
Yes, I think she feels honored that people are
going to recognize her efforts.

PG 136   PG 137

After Viewing Pages 136 and 137

❶ Understand: Viewing; Identifying—Where
Look at the picture. Can you find Judy? Where is she sitting?
(She is sitting in the front row.)

❷ Apply: Inferring; Explaining; Using Vocabulary—
thrilled, curious, honor
How do you think she feels?
(She is thrilled and excited about representing her class. She is honored. She is nervous. She is curious to find out what the class would get . . .)

STORY READING INSTRUCTIONS

Students read pages 138–144 without the teacher, independently or with partners.

COMPREHENSION PROCESSES

Understand, Apply, Evaluate

PROCEDURES FOR READING ON YOUR OWN

1. **Getting Ready**

   Have students turn to page 138.

2. **Setting a Purpose**

   Explaining—Action; Inferring; Responding

   Before students begin reading, say something like:
   As you read, think about the answers to these questions:
   - What happened at the school assembly?
   - Did this story have a happy ending? Why or why not?
   - Would you recommend this book to a friend? Why or why not?

3. **Reading on Your Own: Partner or Whisper Reading**
   - Have students take turns reading every other page with a partner or have students whisper read pages 138–144 on their own.
   - Continue having students track each word with their fingers.

4. **Comprehension and Skill Work**

   Tell students that after they read on their own, they will do Comprehension and Skill Activity 12, write a letter to Judy Moody, and do the Many Faces of Judy Moody for this chapter. Guide practice, as needed. (For teacher directions, see pages 133 and 134.)

5. **Homework 11: New Passage**

> **PREP NOTE**
>
> **Setting a Purpose**
>
> Write questions on a chalkboard, white board, or large piece of paper before working with your small group.

PG **145**

STORY COMPREHENSION

COMPREHENSION PROCESSES

Understand, Analyze

WRITING TRAITS

Conventions—Period

Identifying—What

Using Graphic Organizer
Explaining—Events
Using Vocabulary—mood

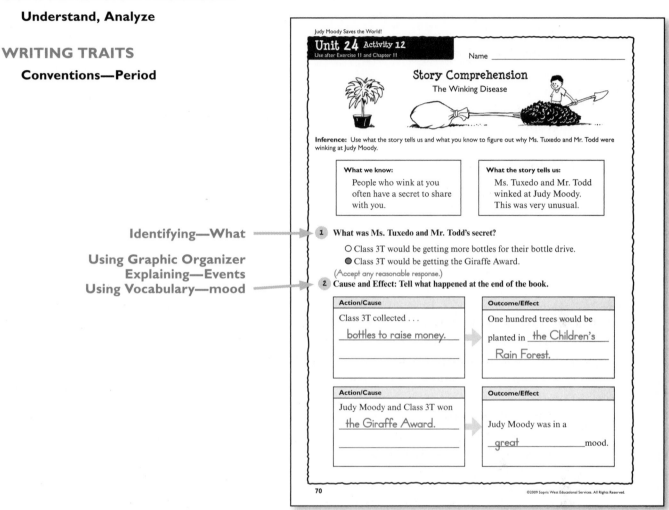

Judy Moody Saves the World!

Unit 24 Activity 12
Use after Exercise 11 and Chapter 11

Name _____

Story Comprehension
The Winking Disease

Inference: Use what the story tells us and what you know to figure out why Ms. Tuxedo and Mr. Todd were winking at Judy Moody.

What we know:	What the story tells us:
People who wink at you often have a secret to share with you.	Ms. Tuxedo and Mr. Todd winked at Judy Moody. This was very unusual.

1 **What was Ms. Tuxedo and Mr. Todd's secret?**

○ Class 3T would be getting more bottles for their bottle drive.

● Class 3T would be getting the Giraffe Award.

(Accept any reasonable response.)

2 **Cause and Effect: Tell what happened at the end of the book.**

Action/Cause		Outcome/Effect
Class 3T collected . . . _bottles to raise money._	→	One hundred trees would be planted in _the Children's Rain Forest._

Action/Cause		Outcome/Effect
Judy Moody and Class 3T won _the Giraffe Award._	→	Judy Moody was in a _great_ mood.

70

©2009 Sopris West Educational Services. All Rights Reserved.

PROCEDURES

For each step, demonstrate and guide practice, as needed. Then have students complete the page independently.

1. **Answering Questions: Selection Response—Basic Instructions** (Item 1)
   Have students read the sentence, then fill in the bubble with the correct answer.

2. **Cause and Effect: Sequence Chart, Sentence Completion—Basic Instructions** (Item 2)
   Have students read the sentence starters, then complete the sentences in each box to explain the cause-and-effect events. Remind them to look back in their books if they need to. Remind students to end sentences with a period.

Self-monitoring
Have students read the sentences to see if they make sense.

ENTRIES 11a, 11b

COMPREHENSION PROCESSES

Understand, Apply, Evaluate, Create

WRITING TRAITS

Ideas and Content
Word Choice
Conventions—Complete Sentence, Capital, Period
Presentation

SPECIAL NOTE

Your students will complete a Dear Judy Moody book. For ease of use, pull pages 47–58 from *Activity Book 4*. Staple the pages together into a book.

PROCEDURES

Have students complete the page independently. Guide practice, only as needed.

Letter Writing: Creative Writing—Specific Instructions (Entry 11a)
Have students fill in the blanks to complete a letter to Judy Moody.
Remind them to start sentences with a capital and end with a period.

Cover: Illustrating—Specific Instructions (Entry 11b)
Have students find the box labeled Entry 11b on the cover and draw a face that shows Judy's mood at the end of this chapter. Remind them to look back in their book, if needed.

Explaining
Generating Ideas
Responding
Sentence
Completion
Sentence Writing

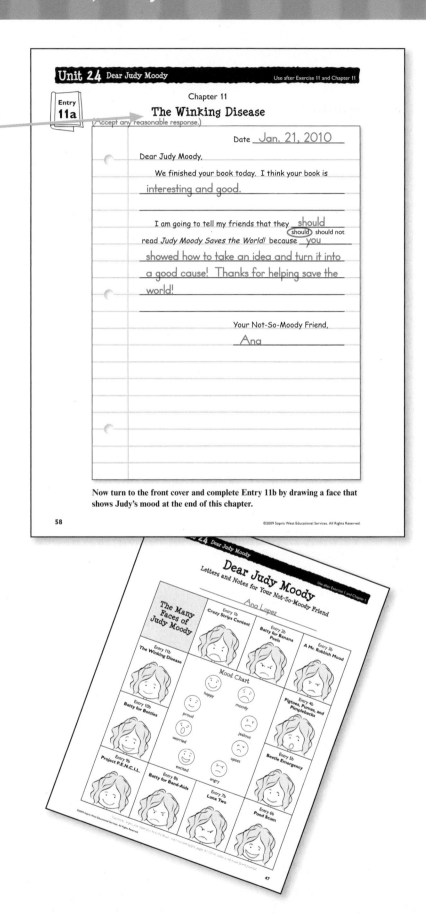

Unit 24 Dear Judy Moody — Use after Exercise 11 and Chapter 11

Chapter 11

Entry
11a

The Winking Disease
(Accept any reasonable response.)

Date **Jan. 21, 2010**

Dear Judy Moody,

We finished your book today. I think your book is
interesting and good.

I am going to tell my friends that they **should**
(should) should not
read *Judy Moody Saves the World!* because **you**
showed how to take an idea and turn it into
a good cause! Thanks for helping save the
world!

Your Not-So-Moody Friend,
Ana

Now turn to the front cover and complete Entry 11b by drawing a face that
shows Judy's mood at the end of this chapter.

58

©2009 Sopris West Educational Services. All Rights Reserved.

Dear Judy Moody
Letters and Notes for Your Not-So-Moody Friend
Ana Lopez

The Many Faces of Judy Moody	Entry 1b Crazy Strips Contest	Entry 2b Batty for Banana Peels	Entry 3b A Mr. Rubbish Mood
Entry 11b The Winking Disease	Mood Chart		Entry 4b Pigtoes, Pumas, and Pimplebacks
Entry 10b Batty for Bottles			Entry 5b Beetle Emergency
Entry 9b Project P.E.N.C.I.L.	Entry 8b Batty for Band-Aids	Entry 7b Luna Two	Entry 6b Pond Scum

47

135

❶ SHIFTY WORDS

Have students read the words. Use the words in sentences, as needed.

❷ SOUND PRACTICE

- For each task, have students spell and say the focus sound in the gray bar.
- Next, have students read each underlined sound, the word, then the whole column.
- Repeat with each column, building accuracy first, then fluency.

❸ ACCURACY AND FLUENCY BUILDING

- For each task, have students say any underlined part, then read the word.
- Set a pace. Then have students read the whole words in each task and column.
- Provide repeated practice, building accuracy first, then fluency.

A1. Rhyming Words

> Have students read each set of words and identify what's the same about them.

C1. Multisyllabic Words

> Have students read each whole word. Use each word in a sentence, as needed.

D2. Related Words

> Tell students these words are related in meaning. They all have to do with what kind of foods animals eat. Have students read the words. Use the words in sentences, as needed.

E1. Tricky Words

- For each Tricky Word, have students use the sounds and word parts they know to silently sound out the word. Use the word in a sentence to help with pronunciation.

species	The humpback whale is a . . . *species.*
unique	Every plant and animal on Earth is . . . *unique.*
chorus	I couldn't remember most of the song, but I remembered the . . . *chorus.*
rhyme	*Treasure, measure,* and *pleasure* . . . *rhyme.*
crustacean	I think lobster is a yummy . . . *crustacean.*
lose	What are you looking for? What did you . . . *lose?*
losing	Some animals are becoming endangered because they are . . . *losing* . . . habitat.

- Have students go back and read the whole words in the column.

❹ ENDANGERED SPECIES

- Tell students these are the names of endangered species they have read about in the story.
- Have students use the sounds and word parts they know to figure out the words. Assist, as needed.

❺ MORPHOGRAPHS AND AFFIXES

- Have students read the underlined part, then the whole word.
- Repeat practice with whole words, mixing group and individual turns. Build accuracy, then fluency.

SHIFTY WORDS CORRECTION PROCEDURE

If students make an error, put the word on the board. Underline the incorrect sound.

Have students identify the difficult sound, then sound the word out smoothly. Have students read the row again. Return to the difficult word for three correct responses.

MULTISYLLABIC WORDS CORRECTION PROCEDURE

If students make an error, put the word on the board. Draw loops under each syllable and guide practice with your hand. Have students say each syllable, then read the whole word.

Fluency

Unit 24 Exercise 12
Use before Who Am I?

1. SHIFTY WORDS Have students read the words.

stink	blink	blank	plank	place

2. SOUND PRACTICE In each column, have students spell and say the sound. Next, have students read the whole column.

aw	ow as in snow	oi	oa
crawl	known	choice	throat
dawdle	hollow	poison	coast
claws	bellow	moist	roam

3. ACCURACY/FLUENCY BUILDING For each column, have students say any underlined part, then read each word. Next, have them read the column.

A1 Rhyming Words	B1 Word Endings	C1 Multisyllabic Words	D1 Compound Words	E1 Tricky Words
riddle	<u>healthy</u>	habitat	seashell	species
middle	<u>complicated</u>	nature	gumball	unique
fiddle	<u>decay</u>ing	continent	humankind	chorus
	<u>contributed</u>	endangered	brainstorm	rhyme
litter	<u>gazillions</u>	medicine		crustacean
bitter	<u>complaini</u>ng	global	**D2** Related Words	
glitter		treasure	herbivore	lose
		extinct	omnivore	losing
			carnivore	

4. ENDANGERED SPECIES Have students use the sounds and word parts they know to figure out the words.

Shenandoah salamander	Dismal Swamp shrew	shortnose sturgeon

5. MORPHOGRAPHS AND AFFIXES Have students read each underlined part, then the word.

natura<u>lly</u>	recogniz<u>able</u>	pollu<u>tion</u>	environ<u>ment</u>

FLUENCY PASSAGE INSTRUCTIONS

This Story Reading targets fluency as the primary goal of instruction and practice.

Students do repeated readings of this passage to improve accuracy, expression, and rate.

Note: The fluency passage is found in *Exercise Book 4*, Unit 24, Fluency, on p. 68.

PROCEDURES

1. **Warm-Up: Partner Reading or Whisper Reading**

   Before beginning group Story Reading, have students finger track and partner or whisper read the selection.

2. **First Reading**

   • Mix group and individual turns, independent of your voice.
   Have students work toward a group accuracy goal of 0–6 errors. Quietly keep track of errors made by all students in the group.

   • After reading the story, practice any difficult words.
   Reread the story if students have not reached the accuracy goal.

3. **Second Reading, Short Passage Practice: Developing Prosody**

   • Demonstrate reading the first paragraph with expression and fluency. Have students finger track as you read.

   • Have students choral read the first paragraph. Encourage reading with expression and fluency.

   • Repeat with second paragraph.

4. **Third Reading, Group Timed Readings: Repeated Reading**

    • Select a page. Encourage each child to work for a personal best. Have students whisper read for a one-minute Timed Reading. Tell students to go back to the top of the page and keep reading until the minute is up.

   • Have students put their finger on the last word they read and count the number of words read correctly in one minute.

   • Have students do a second Timed Reading of the same page.

   • Have students try to beat their last score.

   • Celebrate improvements.

5. **Written Assessment (Comprehension and Skill)**

   Tell students they will do a Written Assessment after they read "Who Am I?" (For teacher directions, see pages 141–143.)

6. **Homework 12: Repeated Reading**

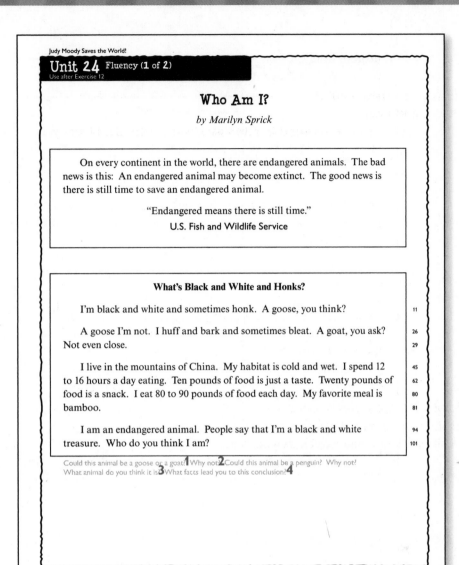

Judy Moody Saves the World!

Unit 24 Fluency (1 of 2)
Use after Exercise 12

Who Am I?

by Marilyn Sprick

On every continent in the world, there are endangered animals. The bad news is this: An endangered animal may become extinct. The good news is there is still time to save an endangered animal.

"Endangered means there is still time."
U.S. Fish and Wildlife Service

What's Black and White and Honks?

I'm black and white and sometimes honk. A goose, you think?　11

A goose I'm not. I huff and bark and sometimes bleat. A goat, you ask?　26
Not even close.　29

I live in the mountains of China. My habitat is cold and wet. I spend 12　45
to 16 hours a day eating. Ten pounds of food is just a taste. Twenty pounds of　62
food is a snack. I eat 80 to 90 pounds of food each day. My favorite meal is　80
bamboo.　81

I am an endangered animal. People say that I'm a black and white　94
treasure. Who do you think I am?　101

Could this animal be a goose or a goat? **1** Why not? **2** Could this animal be a penguin? Why not?
What animal do you think it is? **3** What facts lead you to this conclusion? **4**

　57

COMPREHENDING AS YOU GO

❶ **Understand:** Explaining　(No, it says it is not a goose or a goat.)

❷ **Analyze:** Drawing Conclusions　(No, it lives in China, not Antarctica. It lives in the mountains, not near the ocean. It likes to eat bamboo, not fish . . .)

❸ **Analyze:** Drawing Conclusions　(I think it's a panda.)

❹ **Understand:** Summarizing—Facts　(Pandas are black and white. Pandas live in China and eat bamboo . . .)

Judy Moody Saves the World!

Unit 24 Fluency (2 of 2)
Use after Exercise 12

A Giant Panda, of Course!

I am a giant panda. I bleat when I feel friendly. I bark when I'm upset, | 16
and I squeal when I'm hurt. The people of my country call me a cat bear. My | 33
scientific name means "black and white cat-footed animal." I have become | 45
very rare. Scientists think there are approximately 1,600 of us left in natural | 58
habitats. | 59

When I was first born, I was about the size of a stick of butter. I was | 76
bald, pink, and blind. For two years, my mother had to take care of me. Now | 92
I'm an adult, and I weigh about 300 pounds. | 101

The other pandas and I are very secretive, so it is hard for humans to | 116
study us. I am ten years old. Scientists aren't sure, but they think I am likely | 132
to live for around 20 years. | 138

I love bamboo. It's about the only thing I really like to eat. A bamboo | 153
forest blooms all at once. These luscious plants take 25 years to grow big | 167
enough to eat. Then the forest dies all at once. When the bamboo dies, we | 182
move on. We have to find more bamboo to eat. | 192

People are clearing land to make farms. They are building homes | 203
and cities. There is less and less land for bamboo to grow. I have become | 218
endangered because my habitat is disappearing. People are worried about me, | 229
and that is good. | 233

People all over the world are working together to help me survive. They | 246
are working to protect my habitat—my world, our home. | 256

How many pandas are still in their natural habitat?**1** Why is it hard for scientists to study pandas?**2**

The author tells you one reason that pandas are endangered. What is that?**3**

A panda's habitat is also very hard to protect. The author doesn't tell you why. Can you figure it out?**4**
You may wish to reread paragraph four on this page.

58

COMPREHENDING AS YOU GO

1 **Remember:** Identifying—How Many; **Understand:** Using Vocabulary—approximately, natural, habitat (Scientists think there are approximately 1,600 pandas still in their natural habitat.)

2 **Understand:** Explaining (It's hard for scientists to study pandas because pandas are very secretive.)

3 **Understand:** Explaining—Fact; Using Vocabulary—endangered, habitat (Pandas are endangered because their habitat is disappearing.)

4 **Analyze:** Drawing Conclusions; **Understand:** Using Vocabulary—habitat, protect (A panda's habitat is hard to protect because it takes bamboo a very long time to grow big enough to eat. Then the forest dies all at once, so the pandas have to find a new forest. We would need to protect many forests for a long time so the pandas would always have food to eat . . .)

WRITTEN ASSESSMENT (1 of 3)

COMPREHENSION PROCESSES
Remember, Understand, Apply, Create

WRITING TRAITS
Conventions—Complete Sentence, Capital, Period, Question Mark
Presentation

Test Taking →

Unit 24 Written Assessment
Use after Exercise 12 and Who Am I?

WARM-UP

| Pablo | talons | ducked | gracefully | Costa Rica |

Rain Forest Predator

Jane was hiking through the rain forest. Her mom and dad followed closely behind her. Pablo, their guide, walked in front of them all. He turned to the others and whispered, "Keep your eyes open. We're getting close. The nest is in that large tree ahead."

Everyone was trying to be quiet. The only sounds were their soft footsteps and the light rain falling on the leaves. Jane could hardly believe she was in the rain forest. The air was warm and moist. When she looked up, enormous trees towered above her. The tropical rain forest of Costa Rica was an incredible habitat.

Suddenly a huge gray and white bird swooped past overhead. It held a snake in its giant talons. Everyone ducked. It flew to its nest high in the tree and landed gracefully. Jane's dad quietly took out his camera and began to take pictures.

The predator ignored the staring people and started to eat its prey. "I can't wait to tell the kids at home about this!" Jane thought. "A real harpy eagle! They'll be green with envy!"

continued →

106

©2009 Sopris West Educational Services. All Rights Reserved.

WRITTEN ASSESSMENT (2 of 3)

Inferring—Goal

Describing—Setting; Sentence Writing

Explaining—Middle, Action
Sentence Writing; Paragraph Writing

Identifying—What
Using Vocabulary—predator

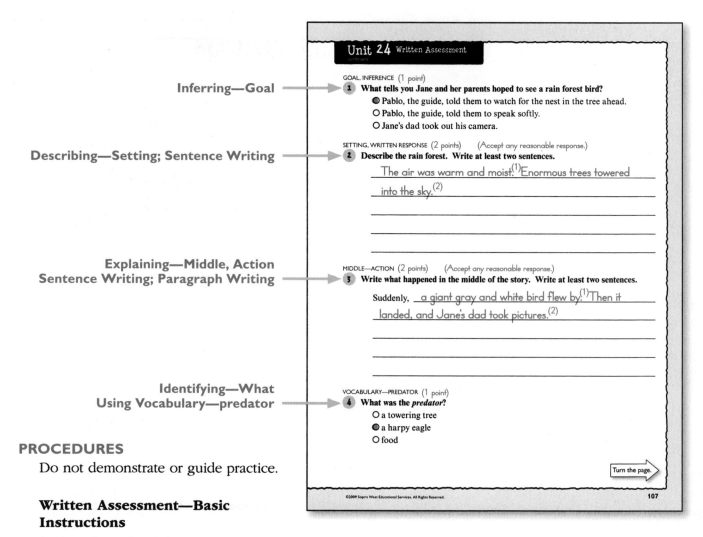

Unit 24 Written Assessment
continued

GOAL, INFERENCE (1 point)
1 **What tells you Jane and her parents hoped to see a rain forest bird?**
   ● Pablo, the guide, told them to watch for the nest in the tree ahead.
   ○ Pablo, the guide, told them to speak softly.
   ○ Jane's dad took out his camera.

SETTING, WRITTEN RESPONSE (2 points)   (Accept any reasonable response.)
2 **Describe the rain forest. Write at least two sentences.**
   The air was warm and moist.[1] Enormous trees towered into the sky.[2]

MIDDLE—ACTION (2 points)   (Accept any reasonable response.)
3 **Write what happened in the middle of the story. Write at least two sentences.**
   Suddenly, a giant gray and white bird flew by.[1] Then it landed, and Jane's dad took pictures.[2]

VOCABULARY—PREDATOR (1 point)
4 **What was the *predator*?**
   ○ a towering tree
   ● a harpy eagle
   ○ food

Turn the page.

©2009 Sopris West Educational Services. All Rights Reserved.   107

PROCEDURES

Do not demonstrate or guide practice.

Written Assessment—Basic Instructions

1. Introduce the Written Assessment.
   - Tell students that their work today is an opportunity for them to show what they can do independently. Say something like:
   You should be very proud of your accomplishments. Remember, on a Written Assessment, you get to show me what you can do all by yourself.

   - Tell students they will whisper read the passage and then answer the questions without help.

2. Check for student understanding.
   Say something like:
   Look at your assessment. What are you going to do first? (write my name)

   What are going to do next? (whisper read the passage)
   What will you do after you read the passage? (answer the questions)

   That's great. Now what will you do if you get to a hard question?
   (reread the question snd try again)
   That's right. What should you do if it's still hard? (reread the passage and try again)
   Very good. And if you still aren't sure, what will you do? (do my best and keep going)

WRITTEN ASSESSMENT (3 of 3)

Using Graphic Organizer (Matrix) Distinguishing—Cause/Effect

Defining and Using Idioms and Expressions—green with envy

Generating Ideas, Asking Questions, Sentence Writing

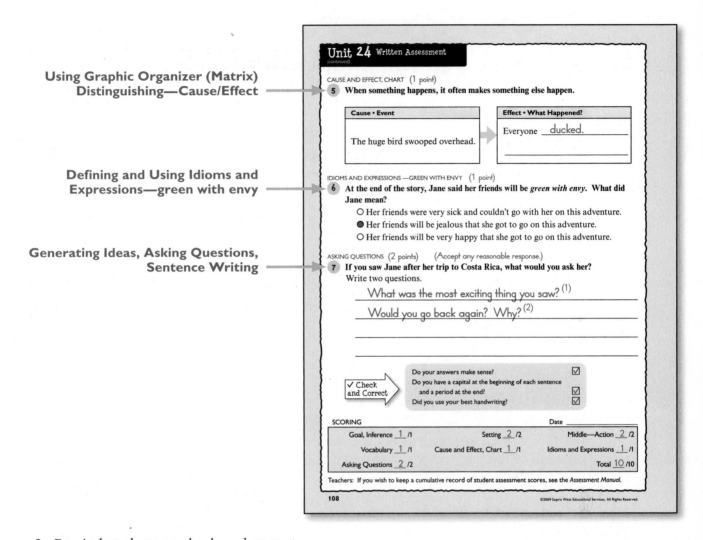

Unit 24 Written Assessment
(continued)

CAUSE AND EFFECT, CHART (1 point)

5 When something happens, it often makes something else happen.

Cause • Event	Effect • What Happened?
The huge bird swooped overhead.	Everyone ___ducked.___

IDIOMS AND EXPRESSIONS —GREEN WITH ENVY (1 point)

6 At the end of the story, Jane said her friends will be *green with envy*. What did Jane mean?

- ○ Her friends were very sick and couldn't go with her on this adventure.
- ● Her friends will be jealous that she got to go on this adventure.
- ○ Her friends will be very happy that she got to go on this adventure.

ASKING QUESTIONS (2 points) (Accept any reasonable response.)

7 If you saw Jane after her trip to Costa Rica, what would you ask her? Write two questions.

What was the most exciting thing you saw? (1)

Would you go back again? Why? (2)

✓ Check and Correct

Do your answers make sense?	☑
Do you have a capital at the beginning of each sentence and a period at the end?	☑
Did you use your best handwriting?	☑

SCORING   Date _____

Goal, Inference _1_ /1	Setting _2_ /2	Middle—Action _2_ /2
Vocabulary _1_ /1	Cause and Effect, Chart _1_ /1	Idioms and Expressions _1_ /1
Asking Questions _2_ /2		Total _10_ /10

Teachers: If you wish to keep a cumulative record of student assessment scores, see the *Assessment Manual*.

108   ©2009 Sopris West Educational Services. All Rights Reserved.

3. Remind students to check and correct.
   When you finish your assessment, what should you do? (check and correct)
   That's right. Go to the top of the page. Reread the questions and make sure your answers make sense. Fix anything that doesn't sound right. Make sure you have an answer for every question.

4. Remind students what to do when they finish their work.

End of the Unit

In this section, you will find:

Making Decisions

As you near the end of the unit, plan to give the Written Assessment and the Oral Reading Fluency Assessment to each child in your group. Use this section as a general guide for making instructional decisions and doing diagnostic planning.

Written Assessment

The Unit 24 Written Assessment is located on page 105 of *Activity Book 4* and on the CD.

Oral Reading Fluency Assessment

The Unit 24 Oral Reading Fluency Assessment is located on page 148 of this teacher's guide and in the *Assessment Manual*.

Certificate of Achievement

Celebrate your children's accomplishments. When your students master the unit skills, send home the Certificate of Achievement.

Goal Setting

Through goal setting, help your students recognize their accomplishments and learn how to be self-directed learners.

Making Decisions

GENERAL ASSESSMENT GUIDELINES

1. After students read Story Reading 12, "Who Am I?", give the group the Unit 24 Written Assessment in place of Comprehension and Skill Work. Follow the instructions on pages 141–143 of this guide.

2. While the group is completing the Written Assessment or any time during the day, administer the Oral Reading Fluency Assessment. Assess each student individually.

   Optional: Graph the results of the assessment. (See Unit 21 Teacher's Guide, pages 100 and 103.)
   • If the student's words correct per minute go up, congratulate the student.
   • If the student's words correct per minute go down, discuss the student's overall improvement and help him or her identify ways to improve for the next assessment.

3. Score oral fluency responses on the Student Assessment Record. Adhere to the scoring criteria in the *Assessment Manual*. Use a stopwatch to time how long it takes each student to read the Oral Reading Fluency Passage, and record errors.

USING WRITTEN ASSESSMENT RESULTS

Results of the Written Assessment *should not* be used to determine whether a student or group of students continues forward in the program. As long as students pass the Oral Reading Fluency Assessment, they should continue forward with the next unit.

The Written Assessment should be used to informally monitor how well students read independently and answer questions in writing. If any student has difficulty with the Written Assessment, re-administer the assessment orally.

If the student has difficulty answering the questions orally:
• Record the types of errors (e.g., main idea, sequencing, open-ended response).
• Provide explicit instruction for these types of questions during reading group, before independent work, and in tutorials, as needed.
  1) Demonstrate (or model) appropriate responses, guide practice, and provide opportunities for independent practice.
  2) For inferential questions, think aloud with students—explain how you arrive at an answer.
  3) For literal questions, teach students to reread a passage, locate information, reread the question, and respond.

USING THE ORAL READING FLUENCY RESULTS

At the end of each unit, you will need to make decisions regarding student progress. Should students go forward in the program? Does the group need extra practice before proceeding? Do individuals require more assistance and practice to continue working in their group? These decisions all require use of the oral reading fluency data and professional judgment. As you analyze assessment results, watch for trends and anomalies.

See the *Assessment Manual* for detailed information and instructional recommendations. General guidelines and recommendations follow:

Strong Pass ≥ 131 WCPM 0–2 errors	• Continue with the current pace of instruction. • Have students set goals. (Until students are reading approximately 180 words correct per minute, oral reading fluency continues to be an instructional goal.)
Pass 110–130 WCPM 0–2 errors	• Continue with the current pace of instruction. Consider increasing fluency practice.
No Pass ≤ 109 WCPM	• If a child scores a No Pass but has previously passed all assessments, you may wish to advance the student to the next unit, then carefully monitor the student. • If a child scores a No Pass but has previously passed all assessments, you may wish to advance the student to the next unit and also provide additional practice opportunities. (See below.) • If a child scores two consecutive No Passes or periodic No Passes, additional practice must be provided. (See below.) • If a child scores three consecutive No Passes, the student should be placed in a lower-performing group.

RED FLAG
A No Pass is a red flag. A mild early intervention can prevent an intense and time-consuming intervention in the future.

Added Practice Options for Groups

Warm-Ups:

• Begin each lesson with Partner Reading of the previous day's homework.

• Begin each lesson with a five-minute Fluency Booster. Place copies of the Unit 20–23 *Read Well* Homework in three-ring notebooks. Each day, have students begin Finger Tracking and Whisper Reading at Unit 20, Homework 1. At the end of five minutes, have students mark where they are in their notebooks. The next day, the goal is to read farther.

• Begin each Story Reading with a review of the previous day's story.

• After reading the story, include Short Passage Practice on a daily basis.

Jell-Well Reviews: A Jell-Well Review is the *Read Well* term for a review of earlier units. A Jell-Well Review is a period of time taken to celebrate what children have learned and an opportunity to firm up their foundation of learning. To complete a Jell-Well Review, take the group back to the last unit for which all students scored Strong Passes. Then quickly cycle back up. See the *Assessment Manual* for how to build a Jell-Well Review.

Added Practice Options for Individual Students

Tutorials: Set up five-minute tutorials on a daily basis with an assistant, trained volunteer, or cross-age tutor. Have the tutor provide Short Passage Practice and Timed Readings.

Double Dose: Find ways to provide a double dose of *Read Well* instruction.
• Have the student work in his or her group *and* a lower-performing group.
• Have an instructional assistant, older student, or parent volunteer preview or review lessons.
• Preview new lessons or review previous lessons.

END-OF-THE-UNIT CELEBRATION

When students pass the Oral Reading Fluency Assessment, celebrate with the Certificate of Achievement on page 149.

Note: Using the Flesch-Kincaid Grade Level readability formula, the Unit 24 Assessment has a 3.4 readability level. Readabilities are based on number of words per sentence and number of syllables per word. Adding one or two multisyllabic words can increase readability by a month or two. Though we are attending to readability for the assessments, the overriding factor is decodability.

GOAL SETTING

Goal setting is a powerful tool to help children be active participants in the learning process. You may choose to have students do goal setting on a regular basis or periodically to boost motivation. If you choose to have students set goals, copy a goal-setting form from page 150 for each student. As students complete their Oral Reading Fluency Assessment, you may wish to say something like:

[Samantha], you read very well! Let's fill out a goal-setting form. It will tell what you are proud of doing in Unit 24 and what you hope to accomplish in Unit 25.

I'm proud of you because you did such a great job in your Dear Judy Moody book. What are you especially proud of? (I've never read such a long book before . . .)

Let's figure out what to write on your goal-setting form. It says "I am proud because I . . . " What would you like me to write? "I am proud because I read a long and difficult book." **Complete the first line of the goal-setting form for the student.**

The next line says, "My goal for Unit 25 is to read . . . " **Fill in the numbers for the student.**

Follow my finger and read the next part of the form.
(I will do my best in reading group, read and reread my stories, read my homework.)
I think you will meet your goal! We'll work together. Maybe you can even beat your goal in Unit 25.

Help students be in control of their progress by helping them identify what actions they can take to meet their goals. Have students sign the goal-setting form to formalize the goal-setting process.

TRICKY WORD and FOCUS SKILL WARM-UP

ecosystem	endangered	recycle	heroine	determined

ORAL READING FLUENCY PASSAGE

A Rain Forest Heroine

★ Jane is in the second grade. She wrote a report about 11
the rain forest. She entered the report in a contest. Jane didn't 23
think she would win, but she did! The prize was a trip to the rain 38
forest. She went on the trip with her parents. 47

Jane got to see an ecosystem that is very different from the 59
forest near her home. She thought the rain forest was beautiful. 70
She went hiking and swimming. She went on a boat trip down a 83
river. She saw many endangered plants and animals. 91

When Jane returned home, she wanted to do even more 101
to help heal the Earth. She helped her family and friends recycle. 113
She did the same thing at school. She raised money to buy land 126
in the rain forest. 130

Jane wants to be a scientist someday and help save the 141
animals and plants. She is determined to study hard and learn 152
everything she can about the rain forest. 159

ORAL READING FLUENCY	Start timing at the ★. Mark errors. Make a single slash in the text (/) at 60 seconds. Have the student complete the passage. If the student completes the passage in less than 60 seconds, have the student go back to the ★ and continue reading. Make a double slash (//) in the text at 60 seconds.
WCPM	Determine words correct per minute by subtracting errors from words read in 60 seconds.
STRONG PASS	The student scores no more than 2 errors on the first pass through the passage and reads 131 or more words correct per minute. Proceed to Unit 25.
PASS	The student scores no more than 2 errors on the first pass through the passage and reads 110 to 130 words correct per minute. Proceed to Unit 25.
NO PASS	The student scores 3 or more errors on the first pass through the passage and/or reads 109 or fewer words correct per minute. Provide added fluency practice. For 2 or 3 days, reteach an exercise page and use a homework passage for fluency practice, then retest.

Certificate of Appreciation

_____

has successfully completed

Read Well 2 Unit 24 • Judy Moody Saves the World!

with _____ words correct per minute.

Teacher Signature _____

Date _____

Certificate of Appreciation

_____

has successfully completed

Read Well 2 Unit 24 • Judy Moody Saves the World!

with _____ words correct per minute.

Teacher Signature _____

Date _____

Goal Setting

I am proud because I _____

My goal for Unit 25 is to read _____ (two words per minute faster).

To reach my goal, I will:

- Do my best in reading group.

- Read and reread my stories.

- Read my homework.

My Personal Best:

In Unit 24, my fluency was _____.

Since the beginning of the year, my fluency has improved by _____ !

Signed _____

Date _____

Goal Setting

I am proud because I _____

My goal for Unit 25 is to read _____ (two words per minute faster).

To reach my goal, I will:

- Do my best in reading group.

- Read and reread my stories.

- Read my homework.

My Personal Best:

In Unit 24, my fluency was _____.

Since the beginning of the year, my fluency has improved by _____ !

Signed _____

Date _____